Stepping In

A Substitute's Guide to Managing Classroom Behavior

Randy Sprick, Ph.D.

THE PERFECT
COMPANION
TO THE CHAMPS
CLASSROOM!

Published in the United States by
Pacific Northwest Publishing
21 West 6th Avenue
Eugene, Oregon 97401
www.pacificnwpublish.com

ISBN: 978-1-59909-032-0

Cover and book design by Hannah Bontrager
Book design and layout by Natalie Conaway
Artwork from clipart.com. © 2009 Jupiterimages Corporation.
Cartoons from www.cartoonstock.com.

Pacific
Northwest
Publishing

Eugene, Oregon | www.pacificnwpublish.com

ABOUT *the* AUTHOR

Randall S. Sprick, Ph.D., has worked as a paraprofessional, teacher, and teacher trainer at the elementary and secondary levels. Author of a number of widely read books on behavior and classroom management, Dr. Sprick is director of *Safe & Civil Schools*, a consulting company that provides inservice programs throughout the country. Each year, he conducts workshops for more than 20,000 teachers and administrators. He and his trainers work with numerous large and small school districts on longitudinal projects to improve student behavior and motivation. Dr. Sprick was the recipient of the 2007 Council for Exceptional Children (CEC) Wallin Lifetime Achievement Award.

ACKNOWLEDGMENTS

Special thanks to:

Susan Ayers

Mickey Garrison

Joe Kasik

Tom Maloney

Linda McLean

Stan Paine

Janet Posenjak

Jean Van Moorlehem

TABLE *of* CONTENTS

PREFACE

*T*he basis of this program for substitute teachers is the proactive, positive, and instructional approach to student behavior management advocated by the *Safe & Civil Schools* series of books and videos. The keystone book, *CHAMPS: A Proactive and Positive Approach to Classroom Management* (2nd ed.), sets forth an approach to classroom management that focuses on preventing problems instead of constantly dealing with them. The book gives classroom teachers the tools to build collaborative relationships with students and provide them with meaningful, positive feedback to enhance motivation and performance. CHAMPS emphasizes the need to:

- Teach expectations at the beginning of the year.

- Review expectations as necessary throughout the year.

- Treat misbehavior as an opportunity to teach replacement behavior.

By following the effective, research-based practices outlined in CHAMPS, teachers develop methods for clearly communicating their expectations for every classroom activity and transition. The expectations to clarify are:

C	**Conversation**	Can students talk to each other during this activity or transition?
H	**Help**	How can students get questions answered during this activity or transition? How do they get your attention?
A	**Activity**	What is the task/objective of this activity or transition? What is the expected end product?
M	**Movement**	Can students move about during this activity or transition? (For example, are they allowed to get up to sharpen a pencil?)
P	**Participation**	What does appropriate student work behavior for this activity or transition look and sound like? How do students show that they are participating fully?
S	**Success**	Soar to success!

The philosophy woven throughout all the *Safe & Civil Schools* materials is symbolized by the acronym STOIC. The word *stoic* describes someone who shows admirable patience and endurance in the face of adversity—such as a caring teacher striving to motivate a difficult student. STOIC stands for five variables a teacher can work with to guide students toward the goal of model behavior. The five variables are:

S **Structure** (organize) your classroom to prompt responsible student behavior. The way a setting is structured has a huge impact on the behavior and attitude of people in that setting.

T **Teach** your expectations regarding how to behave responsibly (i.e., be successful) within the structure that you have created. Sports coaches provide a great example of teaching behavior and re-teaching as needed to help each individual achieve full potential.

O **Observe** whether students are meeting expectations (monitor!). In the short run, this means circulate and visually scan the classroom. In the long run, this means collect and analyze data on student progress.

I **Interact** positively with students. Provide frequent noncontingent attention to build relationships. Provide frequent, age-appropriate positive feedback to acknowledge students' efforts to be successful.

C **Correct** misbehavior fluently. This means briefly, calmly, consistently, immediately, and (as much as possible) privately.

- Brief corrections maintain instructional flow and reduce the degree of disruption the misbehavior causes.

- Calm corrections model responsible ways to deal with conflict, avoid escalating emotional intensity, and keep your blood pressure at a reasonable level.

- Consistent corrections allow you to be on "automatic pilot" and demonstrate to students that you are fair and equitable.

- Immediate corrections prevent minor misbehavior from becoming major misbehavior.

- Reasonably private corrections model respect and help maintain the student's dignity and your relationship with the student—while still addressing the problem.

STOIC represents an objective yet caring and compassionate program for behavior management. Classroom teachers and *substitute* teachers can greatly influence student behavior for the better. By following the principles of STOIC and CHAMPS, and using the techniques presented in the books, teachers can realize a respectful, positive learning environment where students can thrive.

> EVERYDAY COURAGE HAS FEW WITNESSES. BUT YOURS IS NO LESS NOBLE BECAUSE NO DRUM BEATS FOR YOU AND NO CROWDS SHOUT YOUR NAME. ••• *Robert Louis Stevenson*

INTRODUCTION

> ❝❝*Typical high school graduates have been taught by substitute teachers for more than one full year of their public education!*
> —*Substitute Teachers Caucus of the National Education Association (2003)* ❞❞

As a substitute teacher, you play an important role in the education of children. Most substitutes are well-educated, caring people who are genuinely interested in helping students learn. But even the most well-intentioned and well-educated teacher will accomplish little when the students are out of control! A big part of the substitute's job entails establishing and maintaining a controlled atmosphere in the classroom so that learning can take place. Experienced substitute teachers understand that their job is difficult for a variety of reasons:

- They don't know until the last minute if, when, or where they will be working.

- They frequently go into unfamiliar situations in which they don't know anyone.

- They deal with students who are more likely to misbehave because their regular teacher is away.

- They are often unsure about expected routines and school procedures.

- They often don't have clear instructions from the teacher.

- They don't have the opportunity to develop long-term relationships with the students or staff with whom they work.

Although most members of the school community are aware that a substitute's task is difficult, few (including experienced substitutes) realize just how important a role substitute teachers play in the education process. On average, ten percent of American classrooms are managed every day by substitute teachers (Sykes, 2003).

This means that during the average student's 13 years of basic education (kindergarten through high school), he or she will spend the equivalent of more than one full year with substitute teachers! Given that students spend so much of their school careers with substitutes, ensuring that things go as well as possible is in everyone's best interest.

The goal of this book is to help you develop techniques and strategies for managing student behavior and for making the days you substitute teach more successful, productive, and satisfying. Effective behavior management is not magic. By learning and practicing the skills described in this book, you will be better prepared to prevent most misbehavior from occurring and to more effectively handle the problems that do arise.

Chapter 1 discusses the information a substitute needs to be an effective teacher when he or she goes into a new school and how a school may or may not have prepared for a substitute. Chapter 2 summarizes some critical DOs and DON'Ts—things to do and things to avoid in order to gain the respect of students, establish and maintain your role as the class leader, and respect the classroom teacher's environment. Chapter 3 describes several essential skills for preventing and managing behavior problems. Chapter 4 illustrates four common discipline situations that substitutes face and provides suggestions on how to handle those situations. The Appendix contains blackline master copies of forms described in the book.

I've come to the frightening conclusion that I am the decisive element in the classroom. It's my personal approach that creates the climate. It's my daily mood that makes the weather. As a teacher, I possess a tremendous power to make a child's life miserable or joyous. I can be a tool of torture or an instrument of inspiration. I can humiliate or humor, hurt or heal. In all situations, it is my response that decides whether a crisis will be escalated or de-escalated and a child humanized or dehumanized.

—Haim Ginott

Chapter 1

ALL THINGS ARE READY, IF OUR MINDS BE SO.

••• *William Shakespeare*

BE PREPARED!

> "
> *Whatever level of support the school offers, it is to your advantage to arrive with a set of rules for student behavior.*
> "

Y ou're going into a school for the first time. What should you expect? Some schools may have a district- or schoolwide program to prepare students, classroom teachers, and substitute teachers to work together productively and consistently. These schools present an ideal situation where everyone (students, parents, school staff, and substitute teachers) works with the same information regarding expectations for productivity and behavior when a substitute teacher is present.

At other schools, individual teachers may have taken it upon themselves to prepare for a substitute, but there is no schoolwide policy. In both of these situations, information and support is available to complement the academic and classroom management skills you bring to the school.

At some schools, substitutes will find that little or no preparation has been done for them. Such a situation can be more challenging, but you can still be an effective teacher by preparing properly.

Whatever level of support the school offers, it is to your and your students' advantage if you arrive with a set of rules for student behavior that you are prepared to enforce (that's what this book will help you with), a file of educational activities (more about this in Chapter 2), confidence, and common sense. The last two are up to you!

The following pages show typical information a well-prepared school or teacher may have ready for you, perhaps in a nicely organized Substitute Notebook. If you find yourself in a less-than-ideal situation, use this list to get an idea of the information you may want to ask about.

≫ no. **1.1a**
(p. 1 of 3)

SCHOOL INFORMATION FOR SUBSTITUTE TEACHERS, ELEMENTARY

School: Chavez Elementary   **Phone:** 555-1212

Address/Directions: 1150 W. 4th St. Take Lincoln to 4th and park in lot next to playground. Use entrance by gym. Front office is down the hall to the left.

Contacts

☐ Key front-office personnel: Kaye Sanders (secretary); Charles Ramirez (principal)   **A**

☐ Teachers (and room numbers) who can answer questions: Julio Cortez, Rm. 14 (mentor); Talisha Shaw, Resource Center

☐ How to use the intercom and/or contact another teacher or administrator while in class: On the classroom phone, dial the room number plus zero. In an emergency, call the front office by dialing 601.   **B**

Schedules

☐ School schedule: Morning bell at 8:25; 1st recess 10:00–10:15; lunch 11:55–12:55; 2nd recess (K–2) 1:45–2:00; dismissal at 3:00.

Overview of teacher's weekly schedule and responsibilities, including: **C**

☐ Recess duty: Monday, 1st recess; Wednesday, 2nd recess

☐ Lunch duty: Walk students to cafeteria; after lunch, meet them at rear door

☐ Bus duty: Walk students to bus loading area (near front door) at 3:05.

☐ Other:

☐ Schedule of daily activities and classes: Roll etc., 8:30–8:45; Reading, 8:45–10; Math, 10:15–11:15; Music/PE, 11:15–11:45; Science (MWF)/Social Studies (TuTh), 1–1:45; Lang. Arts, 2–2:40

☐ Assembly schedule and procedures: Assemblies from 11:00–11:55, when scheduled (usually 1st Monday of the month)

Classroom information

Location of: See classroom notebook.   **D**

☐ Lesson plans: See classroom notebook.

☐ Backup lesson plans and activities:

☐ Copy machine (password or key code and copy allotment):   Main office. Ask Ms. Sanders for key code if not specified in classroom notebook.

☐ AV equipment/procedures: Take reservation number to library. Return equipment by 4 PM.

☐ Map of classroom and school: See classroom notebook.

☐ Seating charts: See classroom notebook.

☐ Student roster/information about individual students: See classroom notebook.   **E**

A Contact information is invaluable. Be sure you know who is available to answer your questions. Some schools have a mentorship system in place, in which a teacher is assigned to provide assistance and information to substitutes.

B If you don't know how to use the intercom system, ask. It is usually inadvisable to leave students alone in the classroom, so the intercom (or other communication system) is your link to the front office.

C You will look and feel more confident if, throughout the day, you know where to go and when you need to be there. If you are aware ahead of time that you have lunchroom duty, for example, you can prepare by asking another teacher what you are expected to do. Then you can proceed calmly and confidently to your position.

D Lesson plans are, of course, a priority. After all, you are in the school to teach. Follow the teacher's lesson plans as much as possible, but don't have students work ahead. More about this on p. 25.

E Be sure to review any available information about students' medical, legal, and religious considerations. From a behavior standpoint, it is very important to have seating charts and information about individual students. If students feel they are anonymous, they may think they can get away with disrespectful or disruptive behavior. If they see that you have their names, and you make an effort to learn them, students will feel more accountable for their actions.

STEPPING IN
*A Substitute's Guide
to Managing Classroom Behavior*
Sample

Classroom information (*continued*)

☐ **Students designated as classroom hosts:**   See classroom notebook.

Ⓐ

☐ **Classroom helpers (student teachers, paraprofessionals, or parents who may be in the classroom):**
See classroom notebook. There is also a chart posted on the classroom bulletin board.

Descriptions of classroom routines:

☐ **Attendance procedure:** Take attendance during first 15 minutes of the day. Place attendance sheet on the clipboard by the door. A student aide will pick it up.

☐ **Lunch count:**   Do lunch count after attendance. Record number of hot lunches on the attendance sheet.

☐ **Dismissal procedure:** Check to make sure room is tidy before students leave. Students should put their chairs up on the desks. Excuse walkers first, then walk rest of students in line to bus area.

☐ **Other:** Daily bulletin in teacher mailbox lists all morning announcements.

☐ **Teacher's expectations for grading papers, cleaning room, feeding animals, etc.:**   If I've left an answer key, please correct the work that students handed in. Please clean the blackboard (except for the right corner). Please feed the hamsters before you leave. Food is in the coffee can on the shelf below the cage. One scoop is plenty. Close and lock all windows. See classroom notebook for more details.

☐ **After-school responsibilities:**
Please fill in an End-of-Day Report (found in the back of the lesson plan book). Be sure to note any students who were especially helpful and any who gave you a bad time. See classroom notebook for more details.

☐ **Emergency procedures (e.g., fire drills, medical emergencies, lockdowns):**
Fire alarm: Make sure all students leave the room. If the classroom is next to a restroom, make sure the restroom is empty. Follow emergency exit route to designated assembly area. Do a head count to make sure all students are accounted for. Send runner to check in with vice-principal Wolf. Return to class when all-clear bell (three short rings) sounds. Building Containment: Will be announced on PA. Notify office of any students who are not in the room. Lock doors and windows; close all blinds and shades. Medical Emergency: Call nurse's office (dial 100). Call office if nurse doesn't answer.

Reports

☐ End-of-Day Report form or explanation of how the substitute is to provide feedback about the day's activities

Ⓑ

☐ Copy of substitute evaluation form (administrator or teacher to fill out)

A

One or more students may be designated to be the host for substitute teachers. (Sometimes it's hard to remember that there are mature, helpful kids in school, too!) Such a student can be a big help with the routines and details of running the classroom. However, remember that he or she is still a student and you are the teacher. (See "That's Not How Our Teacher Does It" in Chapter 4, p. 55.)

B

A report that you fill out at the end of the day can tell the classroom teacher what was accomplished and how the students behaved. Also, if students know you will be submitting a report to their regular teacher, it will encourage good behavior. The school or teacher may provide such a form.

If not, you can be prepared with your own blank form to fill out. Copy and complete Reproducible 2.1a, b, or c in the Appendix.

C

If the principal or another staff member visits your classroom, that person is there to help more than to judge you. When there is a school policy of administrator or teacher visits, students know that whenever a substitute is in their class, someone will be checking to see how things are going and whether students are behaving appropriately.

The classroom teacher, an administrator, or another teacher may fill out an evaluation of your performance. This is valuable feedback that you can use to improve your teaching skills. In fact, we encourage you to ask for classroom visits and written evaluations.

STEPPING IN
*A Substitute's Guide
to Managing Classroom Behavior*
Sample

Rules

☐ **Summaries of classroom discipline and motivation/reward systems and any schoolwide discipline policies/procedures:**
Students are expected to behave in ways that don't interfere with the rights of other students to attend class and learn. School rules are posted in the classroom. Assign consequences to students who behave inappropriately. Warn once, tell once, then send the student to the office. Use the PA to notify the office any time you send a student there. School staff are responsible for enforcing behavior standards in common areas (hallways, bus area, etc.). The classroom notebook has info on the reward systems I use.

Policies/procedures for common situations:

☐ **Hall passes:** If a student has a legitimate reason to leave the classroom, fill out a hall pass. The pass must be returned when the student returns.

☐ **Cell phone/pager use:** Cell phones and pagers must be turned off during class.

☐ **Personal electronics use (laptops, MP3 players, etc.):** Music players may not be used during class. Laptop computers may be used for special projects and note–taking at my discretion.

☐ **Restroom use:** Student should raise hand and ask to use the restroom. Issue a hall pass. Only one person at a time should be allowed to leave.

☐ **Drinking fountain use:** Student should raise hand and ask for a hall pass.

☐ **Pencil sharpener use:** Students may use the pencil sharpener when they need to, but must not talk.

☐ **Acceptable free-time activities:**
Drawing (students can ask for paper); reading; homework. Students can ask for books or permission to do a puzzle. When everyone is done working, it's OK to talk quietly to one other student.

☐ **Recess procedures for rainy days:**
An announcement will be made over the PA when students are to report to the gym for recess when weather is bad.

☐ **Recess protocol:**
Line up students and walk them to the playground. Each class has recess equipment in the storage closet. Keep track of what goes out. At the end of recess, students line up by class outside the playground door. Meet them there and walk them back to classroom.

☐ **Students in room before and after school:**
No students are allowed in the classrooms before school. They can leave their things in the hallway. Students must leave classrooms by 3:10 PM. They can study in the library until 4. Close and lock windows before leaving the classroom.

> Write down your basic classroom rules so you are prepared if you don't know the school's or the teacher's rules. You will want to be able to clearly state your expectations for student behavior. This sample form includes examples of some reasonable, unambiguous classroom rules.

A Find out where problematic students should be sent, if necessary, and whether you need to file a report. Not all schools use the principal's office as the destination for these students. Some schools may prefer a team teacher's classroom or some other resource room. Find out whether you need to contact the office before sending a student out of the classroom. However, try to avoid sending students out unless absolutely necessary.

B As you read the list of rules, think of how you would like to handle these situations. If students think you are unsure of the policy for hall passes, for example, they may try to make up their own rules and pass them off as class rules. If you prepare yourself by knowing the school's policy or by having your own policy that you can clearly state, this assures the students that you are in charge.

Reproducible hall pass forms appear on Reproducible Form 1.2 in the Appendix (see example below).

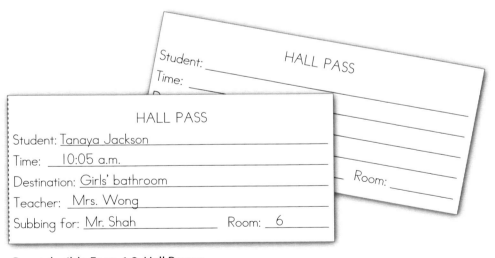

Reproducible Form 1.2. Hall Passes

for long-term substitutes

School information becomes even more important when you take on long-term substituting assignments (anywhere from two weeks to several months). The more time you spend at a school, the more likely you are to participate in fire drills, assemblies, etc. You may also be assigned to regular nonclassroom duties such as supervising lunch, recess, and bus loading. Be sure you know what duties you are expected to perform and what those duties involve. Will you be conducting parent-teacher conferences? Participating in inservice trainings? In the case of planned absences such as maternity leaves, some schools or districts may support a meeting or joint workday between you and the teacher you'll be substituting for. This is a great opportunity to learn the teacher's and the school's expectations. If such a meeting isn't possible, direct any questions you have to the school principal.

Blank versions of the School Information for Substitute Teachers checklist appear in the Appendix. Reproducible Form 1.1a, shown on the preceding pages, is designed for use in elementary schools. Reproducible Form 1.1b is a version more suitable for secondary schools. You can copy either version to use at a new school. That way, you will be ready to take notes if the school has not already prepared for your arrival.

If you find you don't have time to thoroughly review the school's and teacher's policies, your priority should be to learn the following:

- Your key contacts among the teachers and office staff, and the best way to contact them

- The schedule and seating chart for the class or classes, including any important information about students

- The location of lesson plans

take note

If you substitute regularly at the same schools or for the same teachers, you may want to assemble a notebook to hold school and/or classroom information. Take the notebook along with you on each assignment.

Technology in the Classroom

Whether it's the school telecommunications system, the classroom computer lab, or the computerized attendance system, you are likely to encounter many technological challenges during your career as a substitute. Ideally, your district orientation will cover how to use the district phone system, the substitute assignment process, and any standard software used for attendance tracking, disciplinary referrals, and so on.

At the school and classroom level, however, you will probably meet with more variability in the types of technology available and the expectations for using them. Most schools have policies for student cell phone use—ask about that when you check in at the office to start your day. The office should also provide any information you need about security systems, phones, etc. Mentor or buddy teachers are also excellent resources for any questions about technology.

During short-term assignments (lasting a day or two), you may want to avoid using any computers in the classroom (no matter what the students may say). If the lesson plan calls for computer use, make sure you have clear instructions on how to start them and what students should be doing.

As is the case with paper grade books, do not enter any grades unless the teacher you are substituting for instructs you to do so (and how to do so). Likewise, do not use the teacher's computer or check the teacher's e-mail. You should never use someone else's user name and password to access any computer or system.

During a long-term assignment, be sure to discuss any classroom technology issues with the school principal or the teacher you are substituting for, if possible. How are computers used for instruction? Can students use computers during choice time? If there are more students than computers, how do you determine whose turn it is? Make sure you know how to start and shut down, what software students can use, and expectations for your use of e-mail (e.g., to receive schoolwide messages, to communicate with parents).

Get a copy of the school's technology use policy and familiarize yourself with it. If you are expected to use particular systems or computers regularly, make sure you are assigned a user ID and password.

When students are using the computers, especially those with Internet access, monitor them carefully to make sure they stay on task. Move about and check what's displayed on the screen. If you notice that a student has multiple windows open, ask to see what's on the hidden ones. Report any inappropriate Internet access or file downloads.

Finally, limit use of your own electronic devices to the faculty room, and don't use any school equipment for personal reasons.

Notes

Chapter 2

TO BE GOOD IS NOBLE, BUT TO TEACH OTHERS HOW TO BE GOOD IS NOBLER—AND LESS TROUBLE.
••• *Mark Twain*

CRITICAL DOS AND DON'TS

*T*he overriding "Do" of substitute teaching is to treat all students with dignity and respect. In return, you should expect respect from the students (although you may have to remind them of this expectation!). With these principles in mind . . .

Do Be aware that your presence can create unease in the classroom.

Change is difficult for most people, and it tends to cause anxiety. Any day that their regular teacher is not in the classroom is a major change for students. Whenever you go into a class for the first time, realize that the students are likely to be on edge, wondering what is going to happen and what you are going to be like. You can help students deal with their anxiety by appearing calm, confident, and pleasant.

Because student anxiety may stem in part from being worried about their regular teacher, you may wish to start the day by telling the students why you are there. If the teacher is out due to a mild illness, let the students know that it is nothing serious, that their teacher will be fine, and that, if possible, you will let them know when he or she will return. If the teacher is seriously ill, check with the principal about what to tell the students.

Do treat all students with dignity and respect.

Students may also be worried about how you will treat them. You need to reassure the students that they have nothing to fear from you and that you will not let things get out of control in the classroom. The best way to do this is to start the day by explaining that you are there to help them have a worthwhile, pleasant, and productive day. Then show them through your minute-by-minute actions that you are skilled enough to accomplish this. More information about how to treat students will be provided throughout the rest of this book.

Do Check in with the front office.

When you arrive at the school, your first stop should be the front office to check in. Front-office personnel can provide you with classroom keys, directions to the classroom, and other useful information. Some schools may keep copies of teachers' substitute notebooks in the office, while others may have teachers keep copies in or on their desks. Also regularly check the mailbox of the teacher you are substituting for.

Do Greet students at the door.

This is one of the most important suggestions in this entire book. Whether you will be teaching first graders or high school seniors, try to get to the classroom and orient yourself before the students arrive. Then greet the students in a friendly yet businesslike manner as they enter the room. Introduce yourself, ask them to take their seats, and let them know that you will inform them about their teacher's absence as soon as the class period begins. Don't be overly friendly. Students do not want or need you to be their best friend. They want and need someone who will lead the class through a productive and worthwhile experience.

> "
> *Students want and need someone who will lead the class through a productive and worthwhile experience.*
> "

At the same time, you shouldn't be too stern. If you act harshly, some students may feel frightened, while others may view you as the enemy, someone they will want to do battle with throughout the day. Just remember to be friendly, firm, and confident.

Greeting students at the door accomplishes several important things. First, you demonstrate to students that you are interested in them because you care enough to be at the door to greet them.

Second, being at the door as students arrive demonstrates that you are not afraid of them. Unfortunately, some substitute teachers actually are afraid to be with students, a fact that students perceive very quickly.

Third, greeting students at the door gives students a few seconds to mentally prepare for the reality that their teacher is not going to be in the classroom. In elementary classrooms, you should also plan to greet students at the door after each activity the class has left the room for—recess or lunch, for example. That helps maintain the positive tone throughout the day.

Sometimes it is not possible to be in the room to greet students as they enter. Perhaps you weren't called for the assignment until shortly before class, or perhaps you had trouble finding the school. If, for whatever reason, the students are already in the classroom when you arrive, calm yourself before you enter the classroom. Even if you have been scrambling and frantically trying to reach the school, you do not want to walk into a classroom looking or feeling agitated. Instead, enter the room and, if the students are quiet, calmly introduce yourself. Apologize for being late and begin any required housekeeping activities, such as taking attendance. If necessary, ask students how to do those activities.

Do   Develop a file of filler activities.

An effective substitute teacher knows and prepares for the fact that sometimes a teacher does not leave enough work to occupy the students for an entire class period or day. When students are idle, there is a higher probability that discipline problems will occur. The regular teacher may have left some backup plans to draw from, but it is a good idea to come to each of your assignments prepared with ideas for activities that can be used just to keep the students occupied. Figure 2.1 shows some typical filler activities.

PULL OUT A BOOK. DO SOME KIND OF VOCAB. DO A CLOSE READ AND HAVE A DISCUSSION. WRITE A RESPONSE.

FOR MATH: PICK A PAGE, ~~PROBLEM.~~ HAVE ONE GROUP SOLVE A PROBLEM AND SHARE WITH CLASS

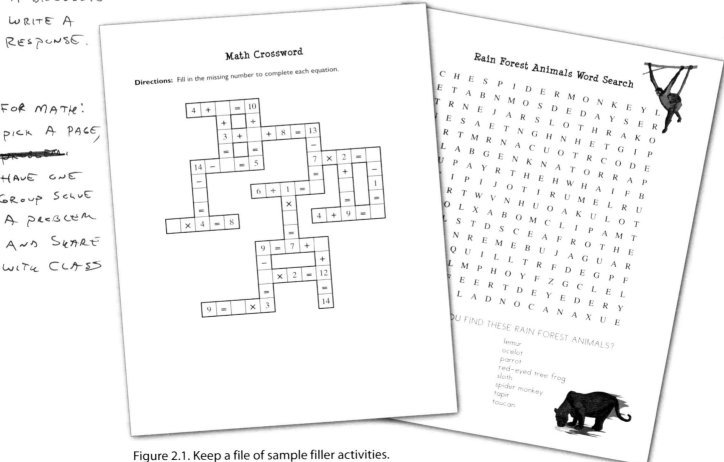

Figure 2.1. Keep a file of sample filler activities.

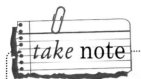

In some schools, the use of the copy machine may be regulated. You may need to ask permission or get a password before making copies, or you may be allowed only a certain number of copies per day.

Also, other teachers may be using the copy machine nonstop throughout the day, and you may find it difficult to interrupt them.

So plan to make copies well in advance of when they are needed. It may be worthwhile to copy a favorite filler activity on your own time in order to be prepared for unforeseen circumstances.

When at schools and in bookstores, keep an eye out for discussion topics, writing assignments, art projects, brainteasers, crossword puzzles, word games, class games, and any other free-time tasks that you can use as time fillers. If you find an interesting worksheet at a school, for example, ask if you may copy it for your file. Whenever you come across an activity that would be easy to use in a classroom, make a note of it. Finally, use other substitute teachers as resources. Ask them about the types of backup activities they use and where they have found good ideas for different activities.

Web sites that offer filler activities for download include:

www.teacherneedhelp.com
www.edhelper.com
www.teachervision.fen.com

Be sure to read and comply with the Terms of Use that apply to any materials you print or download.

Do   Get the students' attention before you speak to the class.

This is especially critical if you can't be there when the students enter the class. If the students are boisterous and you need to speak to the class, ask for their attention in a firm, but not shouting, voice. As you ask for attention, raise your hand in the air and hold it there (Figure 2.2). An upraised hand is a common symbol for attention. Because it is used by many teachers, there is a good chance that at least some of the students will be familiar with this signal, even if their current teacher does not use it. If the students quiet down fairly quickly, thank them for their attention, introduce yourself, and begin the day.

If the students do not give you their attention—that is, if the noise continues—wait. Do not attempt to shout over the noise. When you shout, you give students the message that they do not have to listen to you unless you are shouting. Just wait until they become quiet.

If it takes longer than a couple of minutes, make note of the time, write that time on the board, then continue to wait. Suggestions about what to do next are covered in more detail in the "Class Out of Control" section of Chapter 4.

Figure 2.2.
Raise your hand in the air as an attention signal.

Do   Guard teacher editions of textbooks and answer keys to assignments.

Teachers often keep teacher editions of textbooks or answer sheets to assignments and tests on their desks. If you see such items, put them in a desk drawer or some other place that is not directly visible to students. This is especially critical at the middle and high school levels when students may be feeling more pressure about grades.

If you put books and answer keys away somewhere, be sure to leave a note for the regular teacher about where you put them. Although most teachers will appreciate your caution in putting these materials away, they will not be happy if they have to hunt for them on their return to school.

Do   Lock the classroom door whenever you leave the room.

This is obviously just good common sense, but it is important to remember, even in elementary schools. A related suggestion is that you be careful about protecting your own belongings. Never leave your purse, wallet, keys, and so on in a place where they could tempt a student.

Do   Present a professional appearance.

Your appearance makes an impression on students, either positive or negative. Dress in a manner that communicates your confidence and your belief in yourself as a professional. This does not mean that you have to wear a formal suit, but you should not be too casual.

Some substitute teachers present an appearance that seems to say, "For what I am being paid, I am going to wear whatever I please." The problem is that when your appearance is too casual, it may imply to students that you do not take yourself seriously as a teacher, and they may think that they do not have to take you seriously either.

Sometimes younger substitutes make the mistake of trying to look too much like the students by wearing the style of clothing that is currently popular with the students. Or they may inadvertently look like high school students by continuing to dress as they did when they were college students. However, a teacher (whether a substitute or not) is different from the students. When students think that a substitute is trying to dress like them, they are just as likely to resent that person as to feel some sense of kinship or allegiance.

Your goal should be to dress like the more formal teachers in the district or districts where you will be working. For example, if some of the male teachers wear neckties but others do not, it is probably advisable for you to wear a tie. Women should probably wear dresses or skirts if that's what some of the female teachers wear, even if others wear jeans and tennis shoes. If no women wear dresses or skirts, you should just try to wear something similar to what the better dressed women are wearing.

Regardless of whether some of the regular teachers get by with wearing jeans and a T-shirt, you should present a more businesslike appearance. By dressing like the more formal teachers, you reduce the likelihood that students, teachers, and building administrators will think you are not taking your role in the school seriously.

Do   Maintain your composure and confidence.

No matter what happens, you need to appear calm and in control, even if you do not feel that way. (A little acting ability can be quite an asset for a teacher—actors are often wonderful substitute teachers!) As stated previously, students want a substitute who will treat them well and who will keep the classroom under control. If you appear frustrated, nervous, or angry, some students may feel that you are not doing your job while others will find your discomfort very entertaining. If these latter students find out that their behavior can cause you distress, it gives them a vast amount of power. Therefore, no matter what happens, try to appear calm. Even if you don't feel calm, just act calm and the students will never know what you are really feeling. The following simple techniques can be very effective in helping you relax and maintain your composure:

 ## Breathe deeply and evenly.

In difficult situations, it can be very easy to take rapid, choppy breaths or sigh repeatedly. You may even hold your breath. Any one of those breathing patterns can make you more tense, even to the point that you feel panicky. Therefore, no matter how difficult the situation is, try to force yourself to breathe slowly, deeply, and evenly.

 ## Use self-talk to reassure yourself.

During difficult circumstances, some people tend to engage in very negative self-talk that can actually make the situation worse: "I hate this job. These kids are brats. If the principal walks in right now, I'll never be rehired in this building." The best way to counteract this sort of self-defeating talk is to use positive self-talk. Identify a phrase that works for you and then repeat it over and over in your head during tense situations. Possible examples include:

- No matter what, they will think I'm very calm.

- No one can make you feel inferior without your consent. (Eleanor Roosevelt, *This is My Story*, 1937)

- This isn't so bad—I can make it until 3:00.

- The good news about this assignment is that it is only temporary.

Pause before you speak or act.

The more tense a situation is, the greater the desire to do something quickly. Two very natural responses to difficult situations—to attack or to run away from the problem—are both disastrous when you are a substitute. Before you lash out or run to the office for help, calm yourself down and think about your options. You do not have to act fast. You have plenty of time to take a few deep breaths and ask yourself, "What would happen in this situation if I tried to handle it by . . .?" An exception to this suggestion is when the safety of a child is of concern. Fast action may be necessary if, for example, one child is about to hit another.

You can handle all of the problems better if you stay calm, and it is easier to stay calm when you remain detached.

 Don't take things personally.

When students are challenging you and behaving badly, it is easy to start thinking, "Why are they doing this to me? What did I do to deserve this?" The fact is, you didn't do anything to deserve it, and the students are not doing it to you. It's more likely that they are pushing limits just to see what they can get away with, or misbehaving now because their teacher is overly strict, or just having some fun while their teacher is away. Some of the students may even be misbehaving because of problems at home.

The important point is that you can handle all of the problems better if you stay calm, and it is easier to stay calm when you remain detached. It may be useful to combine this suggestion with the one about self-talk—for example, repeat "I don't have to take this personally."

Do   Fill out an End-of-Day Report.

Students sometimes display the attitude that the work they do for a substitute has no meaning to their regular classroom teacher or effect on their ultimate course grade, so there is no reason for them to do it. This may be especially true for work initiated by the substitute as filler work or for extra credit. If students perceive no purpose to the class, behavior can go downhill fast.

Let students know that you are keeping track of their behavior and their work habits and will be giving their teacher a written report (see examples on the next pages). Go to school prepared with some blank report forms (Reproducible Forms 2.1a, 2.1b, and 2.1c in the Appendix).

(continued on p. 24)

STEPPING IN
*A Substitute's Guide
to Managing Classroom Behavior*

Sample

≫ no. **2.1a**

END-OF-DAY REPORT, ELEMENTARY (Version 1)

Substitute Teacher: David Nguyen

Classroom Teacher: Jennifer O'Malley   **Date:** Tuesday, Oct. 28

Time: 8:15–9:15 **Activity:** Reading **This is what we did:** After introducing myself, taking roll, and talking about the class rules, we started on the day's reading assignment. I followed the "Unit 3, Day 4" instructions in the Teacher's Guide. We went through the exercise, then the kids reviewed what had happened in the story so far. Several volunteered to read parts of the chapter, and we discussed the questions. Keisha explained how you do the partner check. Then we worked on worksheets 7 and 8. Some students still have more to do on 8. **Special circumstances or problems:**	**Absent students:** James Page **Student behavior was:** _X_ Excellent! ____ Average ____ Unacceptable (describe in box at left)
Time: 9:15–10:00 **Activity:** Math **This is what we did:** As your lesson plan indicated, we went over the homework as a class and worked the harder problems on the board. Keisha and Jacob were especially helpful. John had not done his homework. Then I gave them their new assignment and had them work quietly at their desks for the remainder of the period. John, Tina, and Abigail needed a bit of help understanding the fractions. There was some whispering, but overall students worked well on their own. **Special circumstances or problems:**	**Absent students:** James Page **Student behavior was:** _X_ Excellent! ____ Average ____ Unacceptable (describe in box at left)
Time: 10:30—11:15 **Activity:** Arts and Crafts **This is what we did:** The kids were a little wound up after recess, but they were excited to work on their art projects. They continued working on their African face masks. I read them the information you left about the cultural significance of the masks. While some of the papier mache was drying, we looked at pictures of African art in the books you left. **Special circumstances or problems:** I had to remind the class to keep the noise down several times. John and Luis spent more time talking than working.	**Absent students:** James Page LaToya had to go to a dentist appt. so she missed Art. **Student behavior was:** ____ Excellent! ____ Average _X_ Unacceptable (describe in box at left)

Reproducible Form 2.1a. End-of-Day Report, Elementary (Version 1)

STEPPING IN
*A Substitute's Guide
to Managing Classroom Behavior*
Sample

>> no. **2.1b**

END-OF-DAY REPORT, ELEMENTARY (Version 2)

Substitute Teacher: Terry Suvak

Classroom Teacher: Curtis Johnson   **Date:** Nov. 22

Students who were absent (include part-day absences):
James Page. LaToya Anderson missed Art to go to a dentist appointment.

Students who were especially helpful (provide specifics): Keisha volunteered to do some homework problems on the board and quietly told me about some kids who had switched seats (John, Kevin, Matthew, and Tony).

Students who had trouble behaving appropriately (provide details): Kevin was rude and misbehaved all day. He made a rude comment about my weight during opening activities, and told me to "get lost" during math. Matthew and Kevin were whispering a lot throughout the day.

Description of what occurred during each of the main activities of the day (academic work and student behavior):

Activity: Taking roll, introducing myself. Some of the kids tried to change seats and names; it took a few minutes to sort it out. Kevin made some rude comments so I reminded everyone of the "respect others" rule.	**Activity:** Arts & Crafts Students got out their African masks to work on. Everyone (except Keisha and Lee) were so noisy and unruly (throwing things, yelling) that I had to tell them to put everything away early and sit at their desks until lunch.
Activity: Reading The lesson plan wasn't very clear, so I just had the kids read what they wanted to read from the stack of books and magazines in the corner, as you suggested.	**Activity:** Lunch Lunch duty was OK. The other teachers helped me out with a table of noisy students.
Activity: Math We went over the homework problems at the board. Someone threw spitballs at me when my back was turned. Then I asked them to start work on the new assignment at their desks. Most began working, but Kevin and Matthew wouldn't stop fooling around. I was constantly asking them to behave.	**Activity:** Spelling Students handed in their homework (in the blue folder on your desk). Then we went through the day's activity sheet. Most students followed along with me and seemed to like writing the words. Kevin, Matthew, John, and Tony didn't do much work. Kevin purposely erased so hard he tore his paper several times.
Activity: Recess I had to remind everyone to keep the noise down when going out. I had Kevin and Matthew stay in the classroom for a couple of minutes after everyone else left for recess.	**Activity:** Science/Social Studies I had the class take turns reading chapter 4 aloud. Had to remind students to respect one another several times.

Reproducible Form 2.1b. End-of-Day Report, Elementary (Version 2)

STEPPING IN
A Substitute's Guide
to Managing Classroom Behavior

Sample

≫ no. 2.1c

END-OF-DAY REPORT, SECONDARY

Substitute Teacher: Elaine Hernandez

Classroom Teacher: Ahmed Hayek   **Date:** Feb. 24

For each period of the day, please thoroughly describe what was accomplished. Also note which students were absent, which students were particularly helpful, and which students behaved inappropriately (be as specific as you reasonably can). Use an extra sheet of paper for additional comments, if needed.

Period 1:
History (Grade 10). I collected homework. Sharon didn't do it. I handed out the worksheet you left and we did it as a class. Most students were very cooperative. There were about 15 minutes left after that, so they wanted to study for their upcoming test. David didn't study, just sat at his desk. Absent: Jayash Patel

Period 2:
Prep Time. I located the DVD player for 4th and 5th periods—thanks for the heads up!

Period 3:
History (Grade 10). I collected homework from everyone. I handed out the worksheet you left and we did it as a class. This took the whole period, as there was some extra (good) discussion, especially from Sally, Oscar, and Mark. I reminded them of the test coming up. Absent: Ben Cohen

Period 4: Social Studies (Grade 9). I handed out the worksheet and showed the DVD about Indonesia. I stopped the DVD a few times to make sure they were paying attention and answering the questions as they watched. Afterwards we had some discussion—I have been to Sumatra and told them a little about my experience there. Most seemed interested. (Karen made a show of being extremely bored.)

Period 5: Social Studies (Grade 9). The DVD and worksheet took all period for this class. A couple kids (Ricardo and Jay, I think, I'm not sure kids were in their right seats!) made a lot of wisecracks during the video, so I had to stop and get them to settle down. I collected the worksheets.
Absent: Peter Stankowski, Anne Wu

Period 6:
Prep Time

Period 7:
History (Grade 11). These kids behaved very well. They got to work on their reports right away and were pretty quiet when accessing information on the computers. Tom was quite helpful in letting me know how things usually operated in the classroom as far as using the computers, etc.

Comments:
All the homework and worksheets I collected are in the blue folder in the top right drawer of your desk. Hope you are feeling better!

Reproducible Form 2.1c. End-of-Day Report, Secondary

for long-term substitutes

Get in the habit of preparing end-of-day reports regardless of the length of the assignment. The regular teacher will appreciate the detail, and you may forget important information if you wait until the end of the assignment to write a report.

If the teacher has not left a form for you to use, take the initiative and fill out your own form. Most teachers will be appreciative of truthful, constructive information about how their class behaved in their absence. Page 38 provides more ideas about how to use the End-of-Day Report.

Do Introduce yourself to mentor/buddy teachers and teachers in neighboring classrooms.

Seek out and introduce yourself to any teachers listed as mentors, buddies, or contacts in the substitute notebook. Also introduce yourself to the teachers in nearby classrooms. These teachers can be a valuable resource if you have any questions about school or class procedures.

for long-term substitutes

As a long-term substitute, you should expect to prepare lesson plans for your class. This task will be much easier if you can do co-planning with another teacher at the same grade level.

And now for the DON'Ts.

Don't Let the students (or other teachers) know that the teacher left poor plans.

Occasionally you may face the difficult or confusing situation where a teacher has left poor plans and even your file of filler activities is not adequate to meet the needs of the situation. When this occurs, it can be very easy to communicate your exasperation with the classroom teacher to the students. This is both risky and unprofessional. First of all, because the students are more likely to have an allegiance to their classroom teacher than to you, they may resent you for criticizing their teacher. More importantly, it is unprofessional to speak poorly of a colleague in front of students, no matter how justified your criticism may be. Remember, you don't have to say everything you think! Just focus on the tips for staying calm and try to get through the difficult situation as best you can.

Don't Act defensive.

While it's important to project a calm, confident attitude, take care not to go overboard. Sometimes, when substitutes are actually feeling defensive, they seem arrogant to the regular teaching staff and perhaps even to students.

> **Be proud that you are a substitute.**

This may be particularly true for retired teachers who are substituting to supplement their income. These teachers may be accustomed to the level of respect and cooperation they received from most students when they were regular classroom teachers. They may not be prepared for the number of disrespectful or otherwise challenging students they encounter when they are working as substitutes. Students may talk back, refuse to work, or claim you are doing something wrong. Substitutes may be especially defensive about comments such as, "You are just a substitute. What do you know?"

Remember, don't get defensive. Be proud that you are a substitute. "Yes, I am a substitute teacher and proud of it. Now, class, the next activity we will work on is . . ."

Don't Use the teacher's future lesson plans.

When a teacher does not leave sufficient or clear lesson plans, it can be tempting to have the students work ahead of what has been assigned—for example, read the next chapter, answer the end-of-unit study questions for history, or complete the next lesson in math. *Try to avoid letting students work ahead.* It's quite possible that the teacher has plans for those lessons (perhaps even something special), and your actions will cause difficulty for the teacher. Whenever you do not know what to do, pull from your own files of materials to keep the students occupied.

Don't Make up due dates.

If the lesson plans are not clear about when something is due, simply tell the students that they should work as quickly and accurately as they can and that their teacher will inform them of the due date upon his or her return. If you are on an assignment that lasts more than two days and you are not able to contact the regular teacher, ask a building administrator for assistance in determining due dates.

Don't Correct student work unless specifically instructed to do so.

When a teacher leaves specific instructions to grade a spelling test or some math worksheets, obviously you should follow these instructions. However, do not take the initiative to grade or mark papers unless you have been given clear instructions. Teachers often have special criteria for how they grade or mark papers or determine scores. Leave the students' completed work clipped together with a note to the teacher about when you collected it. The teacher can take care of the grading when he or she returns.

for long-term substitutes

Long-term assignments are usually exceptions to the previous two Don'ts. You will most likely be expected to grade student work and record grades in the teacher's grade book. If possible, try to arrange a time to meet with the teacher you'll be substituting for prior to his or her absence to go over grading, classroom procedures, student information, and so on. Also take advantage of any opportunity to observe the teacher and class ahead of time. Likewise, it can be helpful at the end of your assignment to meet with the returning teacher to review your End-of-Day Reports and discuss any issues with grading, student behavior, etc. Be sure to ask administrator approval before scheduling such meetings.

Don't Write in the grade book.

Unless given specific instructions otherwise, assume that the teacher's grade book is off limits. Do not write in it and do not let it fall into the hands of students. A grade book can be a teacher's most important record-keeping tool, and the safest thing to do is to simply leave it alone. This holds true for computerized grade records as well.

Don't Be overly sensitive to unintentional slights.

A number of substitute teachers have indicated that they feel insulted when asked by staff members, "Who are you today?" These staff members are not trying to be insulting. Although arguably a rude question, this is also a quick way for a staff member to find out which of his or her colleagues is out of the building. Simply respond with something like, "I am subbing for Ms. Jefferson, who is out with the flu. My name is Theresa Herrera. How are you today?"

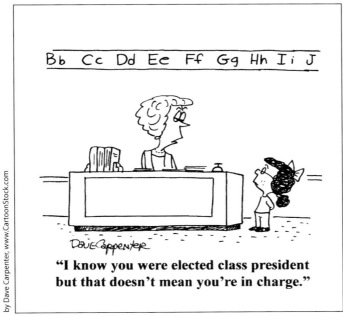

by Dave Carpenter, www.CartoonStock.com

"I know you were elected class president but that doesn't mean you're in charge."

QUICK REVIEW: SUBBING DOS

>> Be aware that your presence can make students feel anxious.

>> Check in with the front office.

>> Greet students at the door of the classroom.

>> Develop a file (or files) of filler activities.

>> When a classroom is chaotic, ask for student attention and wait until you get it.

>> Guard teacher editions of texts and answer keys to tests.

>> Lock the door when you leave the classroom.

>> Present a professional appearance.

>> Maintain your composure and confidence.

>> Fill out an End-of-Day Report.

>> Introduce yourself to mentor/buddy teachers and teachers in neighboring classrooms.

QUICK REVIEW: SUBBING DON'TS

>> Don't let students (or other teachers) know that the teacher left poor lesson plans.

>> Don't use the teacher's future lesson plans.

>> Don't get defensive or act superior.

>> Don't make up due dates for assignments.

>> Don't correct student work unless specifically instructed to do so.

>> Don't write in the grade book unless specifically instructed to do so.

>> Don't be overly sensitive to unintentional slights.

Chapter 3

I LIKE A TEACHER WHO GIVES YOU SOMETHING TO
TAKE HOME TO THINK ABOUT BESIDES HOMEWORK.
••• *Lily Tomlin as "Edith Ann"*

PRINCIPLES OF BEHAVIOR MANAGEMENT

> **Students cannot know what you expect or how you think they are doing unless you communicate with them.**

*T*his chapter addresses five basic principles for effectively managing student behavior.

COMMUNICATE with students.
ORCHESTRATE student behavior during and between activities.
CIRCULATE throughout the classroom.
MOTIVATE students to follow the rules and use their time productively.
CORRECT student misbehavior when it occurs.

PRINCIPLE 1:
COMMUNICATE with students.

Students cannot know what you expect or how you think they are doing unless you communicate with them. Therefore, you should develop a set of reasonable expectations for student behavior. Plan to explain your expectations at the beginning of the day or class period and make a conscious effort throughout the day or in each class to let individual students and the entire group know how they are doing. Stating a few simple rules is the best way to communicate your expectations to students.

 Develop rules.

You should identify three or four rules that reflect how you expect students to behave. These guidelines will give you a behavioral structure for those times when you work in a classroom in which the teacher has not posted rules. Also, the process of developing rules will help you clarify for yourself what your expectations are. Your rules should let the students know the most important things for them to keep in mind during their time with you. Be aware that if the rules are too complicated, or if you have more than four, students may not pay attention when you present them.

As much as possible, state the rules positively. Positive statements of expected behavior provide more information and create fewer problems than do rules that tell students what not to do. Avoid rules that say, "Students will . . ." Rules should be stated in a way that applies to everyone, including yourself. This communicates to students that you will be attempting to follow all the rules in the same way that you expect students to follow them. Following are two sample sets of rules:

---

for example

Middle School and High School Classroom Rules
- Ask before you leave the room.
- Respect whoever is talking.
- Be productive.

Elementary Classroom Rules
- Stop and listen when I say, "I need your attention, please."
- Treat everyone with respect. Treat everyone the way you would want to be treated.
- Work hard.

When you first arrive at a classroom, check to see whether the teacher has rules posted. If you do not see any, simply write your rules on the board near where you write your name. When it is time to begin class, introduce yourself and then present your rules. Give students a little information about why the rules are important. For example, you might tell secondary students that the reason you require them to ask permission before they leave the classroom is that you are responsible for knowing where each student is at all times.

If a teacher does have rules posted, quickly decide whether they are sufficient or whether you need to add some of your own. As much as possible, work with the teacher's posted rules. However, if there is no rule about something that you feel is very important, such as treating everyone with respect, write your additional rule on the board. When you have finished introducing yourself, inform the students that you expect them to follow their teacher's rules while you are there. This is also a very good time to let students know that you may do some things differently from their teacher and that you hope they will be flexible and patient with you. Additional suggestions on this topic can be found in the section "That's Not How Our Teacher Does It" in Chapter 4.

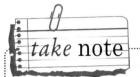

take note

Detailed information on developing a range of consequences for when students don't follow classroom rules is presented later in this chapter under Principle 5, "Correct student misbehavior when it occurs."

   Clarify procedures.

If students ask what will happen if they break a rule, inform them that you will first give a reminder about the rule and what the person should do to follow it. If the person continues to break the rule, you will implement a consequence. At this point, tell the students about the range of consequences you might use.

for example

In a high school class, you might say something like:

"Thanks for that question. If a student breaks a rule, such as the one about respecting the person who is speaking, I will give that student a reminder about the rule and suggest that he or she needs to be more respectful. If the problem continues after that reminder, I will implement a consequence. The type of consequence will depend on how severe the problem is. I might, for example, require the student to stay after class for a minute or two to discuss the situation. I might leave a note for your teacher. If necessary, I might send the student to the office. But I hope I won't have to worry about that because I think we can all follow these few basic rules."

Monitor the class and enforce the rules when necessary.

The best way to enforce the rules is to interact with the students. By looking at, talking with, and listening to students, you will be aware of when students are following the rules and when they are not. Some insecure substitute teachers do not talk to or even look at students unless a student is causing a disruption. This is a problem for the following reasons:

- Students need to feel important and to know that you are aware of and interested in them.

- Paying more attention to misbehavior than to appropriate behavior may actually encourage other students to misbehave.

- If you don't notice and address "minor" rule infractions, students will probably try bigger and bigger infractions to see what they can get away with.

While you are speaking to the class, be sure to make eye contact with students. When you are not leading classwide instruction or discussion, take every opportunity to talk to students one-on-one. Demonstrate that you are interested in and aware of them as people. Ask students their names. Chat with them for a moment or two. Show an interest in their work. Let them know that they can ask you if they have any questions. Do not do this so much that you interfere with their time to complete work, however, and don't try to be their best buddy. Just be what you are: An adult who is interested in, cares about, and enjoys interacting with students.

PRINCIPLE 2:
ORCHESTRATE student behavior during and between activities.

The job of a substitute teacher is similar to that of a band leader or orchestra conductor who is responsible for leading a group of musicians from one piece of music to the next, setting the style and pace of each piece of music, keeping the musicians together so that the individuals function as a group, and so on. You have to lead the students from one activity to the next, establish the behavioral expectations for students within each activity, and keep a group of separate individuals working together as a unit.

> **"**
> *When you praise, describe in a matter-of-fact way what the student is doing.*
> **"**

One thing that can help, if time permits, is to review the whole day's schedule beforehand. Identify when your first break will be—recess, for example. During this time you can organize your thoughts and mentally regroup. Try to develop a mental picture of how each activity will look, sound, and feel up until that break. The purpose of this rehearsal is to give you a sense of what each activity will be like so that you will be more comfortable guiding the students through the tasks and from one task to the next.

---

for example

A mental rehearsal of the schedule and plans left by the teacher might go like this:

I'll meet the students at the door as they enter at 8:05. At 8:10, the first period starts and I will introduce myself, review how my rules relate to the rules posted on the wall, and take attendance. This should take between two and four minutes. Then I will lead students through a review of their math homework by asking individual volunteers to go to the board and demonstrate their answers and how they arrived at their answers. If the class disagrees on any answer, we will work the problem together. Students will correct their own papers, and it is OK if they revise problems on their own sheets. I will end that activity by collecting the homework assignments. This is likely to take ten to fifteen minutes. As this activity ends, I'll give the class feedback about how well they did.

Next, I'll introduce Section 5-6 from the math book, and we will work together on the sample problems. Hallie and James can help with explanations if I have trouble explaining any of the concepts. This will take about five to ten minutes, and I'll wrap up this activity by giving the class feedback about how well they did.

For the remainder of the class period, students can work individually or in pairs on the problems within Section 5-6. Students who have not finished all the problems by the end of the period are to finish them as homework. Those who finish early may study individually or in pairs for a test that is coming up in three days; they should already know about the test. First period ends at 8:50, so about a minute before that I should give the class feedback and instruct them to begin packing up their materials to be ready for me to excuse them after the bell rings. Between first and second period, I will greet students at the door. Second period begins at 8:55. I will . . .

CHAMPS

You may see a CHAMPS poster in your classroom. CHAMPS is an approach to classroom management that emphasizes teaching behavioral expectations for activities and transitions. (It is explained in more detail in the Preface.) By following CHAMPS, teachers are able to give students clear, step-by-step instructions. Familiarize yourself with these guidelines, and you can step into a CHAMPS classroom ready to orchestrate student behavior with a method you know the classroom teacher uses.

*C*onversation: Can students engage in conversations with each other during this activity (or transition)? If yes, about what? With whom? How many students can be involved in a single conversation? How long can conversations last?

*H*elp: How do students get questions answered? How do students get your attention? If students have to wait for help, what should they do while they wait?

*A*ctivity: What is the expected end product of this activity? This may vary from day to day. Or explain the transition. What will be different afterwards (e.g., change in location, use of different materials)? Include time criteria (how long it should take).

*M*ovement: Can students get out of their seats during the activity or transition? If yes, what are acceptable reasons? Do they need permission from you?

*P*articipation: What behaviors show that students are participating fully and responsibly? What behaviors show that a student is not participating?

*S*uccess: By following the expectations for Conversation, Help, Activity, Movement, and Participation, students can soar to success.

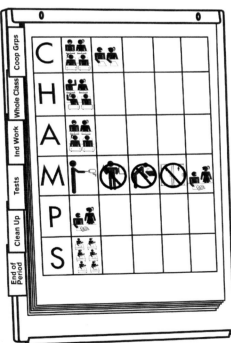

From Sprick, R. (2009). CHAMPS: A Proactive and Positive Approach to Classroom Management (2nd ed.). Eugene, OR: Pacific Northwest Publishing.

As you finish one task or project, inform students what will be happening next and describe to them how you think the task is to be conducted. Do not actually begin any activity until you have clarified for students how they are to behave in that activity. For example, if the class is scheduled to work on the math assignment next, you should clarify for the students whether they should work individually, in pairs, or in larger groups. Also tell them whether they can talk to each other during this time and the deadline for completion (if you know it). *Note:* Do not actually begin any activity until you have clarified for students how they are to behave in that activity.

As you introduce an activity, some students may say, "That is not how our teacher usually does it." In general, if the students seem to be sincerely trying to help, accept their information and modify your expectations to fit what students describe as the usual procedures. If you sense that the students are playing some kind of game or trying to con you regarding the usual procedures, calmly inform them that this is how you want to run the activity and that it is OK if it is different from how their teacher usually does it. More information on dealing with this situation can be found in the section "That's Not How Our Teacher Does It" in Chapter 4.

To summarize, you can and should orchestrate student behavior by beginning each activity with an explanation to students about what they need to be doing. At the end of each activity, tell the students how it went and then inform them about the next activity. This process will increase the likelihood that the individuals in the class will work smoothly as a group.

PRINCIPLE 3:
CIRCULATE throughout the classroom.

As much as possible, be out among the students. Walk around the room in unpredictable patterns (that is, do not always take the same route). This is especially critical while students are working on tasks individually or in small groups. However, it is also a good idea when you are leading discussions or presenting information to the whole class.

Moving about the classroom accomplishes several things. It communicates that you are there for the students should they have a question or otherwise need assistance. It also demonstrates that you are not afraid of the students. Perhaps most importantly, your movement around the classroom increases the chance that students will follow the rules and behave appropriately. Just as adults are more likely to observe the speed limit when they see a patrol car on the highway, students are more likely to behave well when they know that you may be coming by their desks at any moment.

As you walk through one part of the room, continually look at the other parts of the room. In this way, no matter where you are located, you will know what is going on in all parts of the classroom. This technique is called *visual scanning*. You are looking to see whether anyone requires assistance and/or whether anyone needs a reminder about following the rules. This type of scanning also allows you to see how well the class as a whole is meeting expectations. This way, you collect accurate information that you can use to provide feedback at the end of the activity and for the End-of-Day Report you leave for the regular teacher. Even when you are helping an individual student with his or her work, you should look up and get a sense of what other students are doing.

If students are using computers, circulating around the room and visually scanning computer screens is essential to make sure students are on task. It can be difficult to distinguish a student who is writing a book report from one who is playing a video game without actually observing what's on the computer monitor.

Visual scanning is even more important during those times when you cannot move out among the students' desks—for example, when you are presenting information using an overhead projector. Because you cannot be physically close to students in the middle and back of the room during this type of activity, you should plan on making frequent eye contact with these students so that you notice when someone has a question or is having trouble following the rules.

by Aaron Bacall, www.CartoonStock.com

A. BACALL

"I don't need to go to a gym. One of my classroom management strategies is to circulate frequently around the room. I figure I walk three miles a day."

PRINCIPLE 4:
MOTIVATE students to follow the rules and use their time productively.

One of the most effective techniques you have for encouraging appropriate behavior is to use individual and group praise (and with younger students, reinforcement systems) to motivate students to follow the rules and be productive.

 Praise individual students.

Praise can be a powerful tool for creating and maintaining student motivation to behave appropriately. However, effective praise is much more than simply saying "good job" all the time. To truly be effective, praise must reflect the following features:

It's descriptive. To keep students motivated, your praise must provide them with specific information about what they are doing right. That is, you need to describe the positive behavior in which the student is engaged, but not make a judgment about the person. "You are doing a fine job of keeping your attention focused on the math assignment" is an example of descriptive praise. "You are so good" is an example of nondescriptive praise that makes a judgment about the person.

You should avoid starting a praise statement with the words, "I like the way . . ." These words shift the emphasis away from what the student did that was worthwhile and important and place too much emphasis on the fact that it pleases you. Given that you will be in the class only temporarily, pleasing you is probably not that important to the students, especially for students in the fourth grade and beyond. When you praise, simply state the behavior that the student performed well and eliminate the "I like" part of the praise statement.

It's age appropriate. Praise should be appropriate to students' ages. Praising kindergarten students while they are hanging up their coats after recess is perfectly appropriate ("Look at what a fine job everyone is doing. You are coming in quietly, hanging up your coats, and going right to your seats. What responsible behavior!") However, making the same comment to fifth grade students is likely to be viewed by the students as insulting. Age-appropriate praise for older students (fifth grade and above) might address things like "using time wisely" or "keeping attention focused on the assignment."

> *When you praise, describe in a matter-of-fact way what the student is doing.*

It's given in a businesslike manner. When you praise, describe in a matter-of-fact way what the student is doing. Try to avoid embarrassing the student in front of others. Students generally do not want someone gushing about how wonderful they are. However, most can accept a quiet statement that summarizes what they are doing right. Although a few substitute teachers may manage to be emotional or gushy with students and still elicit a good response, they are the exception. You are better off planning to be businesslike rather than emotional when you praise. If you notice that students seem to react to your praise with embarrassment, try being a little less emotional, enthusiastic, and friendly when you praise them and see what happens.

It's given in a reasonably private setting (with older students). With students in the fourth grade and above, use a quiet voice to praise individual students. You do not need to whisper or make the comment a secret, but you definitely want to avoid speaking in a voice that the whole class can hear. You don't want it to seem as if you are praising the student for the purpose of making him or her an example to the rest of the class. Praising one student as a public announcement to the class may brand the student as a "suck up" or teacher's pet. This will not only embarrass that particular student but also likely cause other students to misbehave on purpose so that you will not praise them. Instead, when you praise an individual student, speak to him or her in a way that is audible only to that student and perhaps a few others near the two of you.

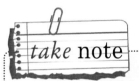

take note

When you praise, don't pause and look at the student when you're done. A pause may imply that you expect the student to respond. A student who is embarrassed may not know how to respond or may respond in a smart or mocking manner.

  ## Give group feedback and use the End-of-Day Report.

Let the students know at the beginning of the day or class period that you will be reporting to their teacher about how they behave during the major instructional activities that occur throughout the day. Then, at the conclusion of each activity, give the class feedback about their behavior as a group before you explain your expectations for the next activity. That is, tell the students how, on average, they behaved.

After giving the group feedback, take a few seconds to make some notes for yourself about what you will report to the teacher regarding that activity. When things go well, tell the class that you will be writing a very positive report about their behavior. When things do not go well, let the class know that you will be informing the teacher about the problems, but during the next activity they will have a chance to demonstrate responsible behavior and thus earn a positive report. Emphasize that despite any problems during previous activities, you are confident that the next activity will be better. When only one or two students misbehave, explain to the class that you will report that the activity went well for most students, but that if individual students continue to misbehave, you may need to include their names in your report to the teacher.

> **_Look for additional opportunities to praise the entire class._**

In addition to the end-of-activity feedback you give to the group, look for additional opportunities to praise the entire class. With primary students, you can praise frequently both for work behavior and for following classroom routines such as coming in and hanging up coats. With older students (grade four and above), focus most of the praise on following rules, working hard, and using time productively. Any praise to older students for following classroom routines should be framed in terms of using time productively. For example, you might occasionally praise a middle school class by saying, "Everyone followed that instruction quickly and quietly. You people use class time very effectively. Now, the next thing we are going to do is . . ."

 ## Use reinforcement systems with younger students.

Reinforcement systems can be very useful in motivating younger students (kindergarten through fourth grade) to behave appropriately. If the teacher you are substituting for has left information about the systems used in the class, continue to use those whenever possible, particularly any set up for individual students. Otherwise, here are descriptions of some of the kinds of systems that may be reasonable for a substitute teacher to use.

SELF-MONITORING

Self-monitoring is a procedure that encourages the students, individually or as a group, to think about, discuss, and record how responsibly they behaved during an activity. The procedure increases the students' accountability because the evaluation forms can be reviewed by the teacher. Copy a behavior evaluation form similar to Reproducible Form 3.1 on the next page onto a transparency (if you have an overhead projector available). At the end of each instructional task, conduct a brief discussion with the students about what rating they think the class should receive for that task. After discussing it with the class, decide for yourself what rating you will give. You might let the students know that you will be leaving this rating form for their teacher to see when he or she returns. Another option is to reward the class for getting good ratings. That is, you might let the students know that for each rating of 3 (all students behaved responsibly), the class will earn two minutes of choice time during which they can choose to play a

Reproducible Form 3.1. How'd We Do? (Monitoring Class Behavior)

STEPPING IN
A Substitute's Guide to Managing Classroom Behavior
Sample

no. 3.1

HOW'D WE DO? (MONITORING CLASS BEHAVIOR)

After each major activity (listed down the left side), circle the number that best represents how the class behaved during that activity.

Time	Activity	Behavior needed improvement.	Some students behaved responsibly.	Most students behaved responsibly.	All students behaved responsibly.
8:15–8:30	Roll call, introduction, announcements	0	1	2	(3)
8:30–8:45	Silent reading, reading interventions	0	1	(2)	3
9:00–9:45	Spelling/writing (Unit 15, Act. 3)	0	1	(2)	3
10:30–11:15	Reading (Unit 15, Ch. 2 and Act. 3-4)	(0)	1	2	3
11:15–11:45	Students went to music room	0	(1)	2	3
12:25–12:45	Read Aloud (Wind In the Willows, Ch. 3)	0	1	(2)	3
12:45–1:45	Math (back-up activity worksheet)	0	1		
1:45–2:15	Science/Social St. (Weather DVD)	0	1		

Notes: Students were excited about special music event, so had trouble focusing on reading activities. After Weather DVD there was no time to start worksheets.

Substitute Teacher: Carrie Johnson

Classroom Teacher: Mr. Higuera

take note

When using Reproducible Form 3.2, first fill in the major instructional activities for that particular class on that day, then give copies of that form to the students.

STEPPING IN
A Substitute's Guide to Managing Classroom Behavior
Sample

no. 3.2

HOW'D I DO? (MONITORING STUDENT BEHAVIOR)

Student: Albert Fontino

Date: March 15

After each major activity (listed down the left side), circle the number that best represents how you behaved during that activity.

Time	Activity	My behavior needed improvement.	I behaved responsibly some of the time.	I behaved responsibly most of the time.	I behaved responsibly all of the time.
8:15–8:30	Roll call, intro, announcements	0	(1)	2	3
8:30–8:45	Silent reading, reading interventions	(0)	1	2	3
9:00–9:45	Spelling/writing	0	(1)	2	3
10:30–11:15	Reading	0	(1)	2	3
11:15–11:45	Music	0	1	(2)	3
12:25–12:45	Read Aloud	0	1	2	(3)
12:45–1:45	Math	0	1	(2)	3
1:45–2:15	Science/Social Studies	0	1	2	(3)

Reproducible Form 3.2. How'd I Do? (Monitoring Student Behavior)

group game or do something quietly at their seats. For every rating of 2 (most students behaved responsibly), the class will earn one minute of choice time.

> At the end of each activity, have each student rate his or her own behavior.

Yet another alternative is to, at the beginning of the day, give each student a form similar to Reproducible Form 3.2. Tell students that at the end of each class period or activity, you will have them record how responsibly they behaved during that period. They will circle a number from 0 (for behavior needs improvement) to 3 (behaved responsibly all of the time). Also tell them that you will be collecting the forms at the end of the day and leaving them for the classroom teacher.

At the end of each activity, have each student rate his or her own behavior. If you use this system, you will need to make a point of checking on students who misbehave during a given activity to see that they do not give themselves a high rating.

If a student does rate himself high, and you disagree, do not argue with the student. Just tell him that you will be keeping your own record of his behavior and that you would like to compare his ratings with your ratings at the end of the day.

Blackline masters of both whole-class and individual student behavior monitoring forms can be found in the Appendix at the back of the book.

STARS ON THE BOARD

One very simple reinforcement and motivational system involves placing a star (or points) on a section of the board under a heading such as "Star Behavior—Everybody is Following the Rules!" At every opportunity you can find when all students in the class are doing what is expected, put a star on the board. Encourage the class to get as many stars as they can by continuing to behave responsibly. The goal is to give out stars frequently so that by the end of the day there are 20 to 30 stars on the board. Then, at the end of the day, allow the students to play a group game as a reward for all the stars they earned.

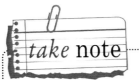

take **note**

When using "Stars on the Board," do not tell the students that each star equals a minute or you will end up having to limit how many stars you give out. That is, 20 to 30 minutes of free time is neither realistic nor instructionally responsible.

GOOD WORK CERTIFICATES

Reproducible 3.3 contains small certificates that can be given to individual students throughout the day for following rules and working hard. A full-page blank blackline master with twelve certificates is provided in the appendix.

You can make several copies and cut out a number of these little certificates. Keep several in your pocket and give them out frequently. Have the students write their names on any certificates they receive and put them into a hat or bowl you have placed on the teacher's desk. Explain that at the end of the day, you will draw one certificate. The individual whose name is on that certificate will earn a small reward. Rewards can be things like a small toy or a certificate for an ice cream cone from the cafeteria (be sure to get approval from the principal). When you use this system, you should give out lots of certificates and make sure that each student earns at least a couple during the day.

> *Good Work Certificate*
>
> *Ana Morales*
> _____
> has done a fine job of behaving responsibly and working hard!

Reproducible Form 3.3 Good Work Certificates

MYSTERY MOTIVATORS

Mystery Motivators is a reinforcement system that is discussed in detail in *The Tough Kid Book: Practical Classroom Management Strategies* (Rhode, Jenson, & Reavis 1992, 1993; second edition will be available in 2010 from Pacific Northwest Publishing). To use it, you need invisible-ink pens, which can be purchased at teacher supply stores or from www.crayola.com.

Although there are many different ways that a Mystery Motivator system could be used by a substitute teacher, one simple method appropriate for a primary classroom is to make a drawing similar to the one in Reproducible Form 3.4 (see the Appendix for a full-page blackline master). In each blank space, write a number with the invisible-ink pen. This number will translate into minutes of choice time at the end of the day. In

take note

If students have not, on average, been successful during an hour in which you are using the "Mystery Motivator" system, do not allow a student to fill in a square to find out what the class would have received. Just go on to the next activity.

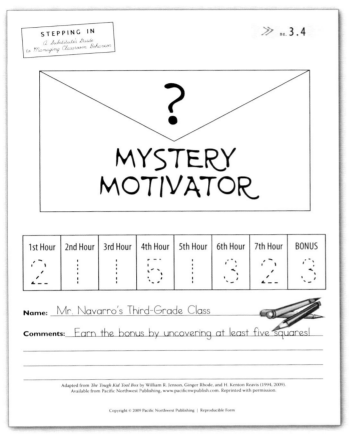

Reproducible Form 3.4. Mystery Motivator

Reproducible Form 3.4, the numbers shown as dotted lines represent numbers that have been written in invisible ink.

At the end of each hour during the school day, briefly share your opinion of the students' behavior for that hour. When the class has for the most part behaved successfully and followed the rules, tell them that they have earned some choice time. To find out exactly how much time they have earned, choose a volunteer to color in one of the squares. The number that shows in the box when it is colored in is the number of minutes they have earned. When creating your own form, keep in mind that only one of the squares should have a big block of time (ten minutes, for example). The rest should be one to two minutes.

Alternatively, you could write numbers with a regular pen and cover them with a removable sticky dot or tape. Have a student remove the tape to see how much time the class has earned.

The power of this procedure lies in its gimmicky nature and in the fact that there is an element of chance—that is, the students do not know ahead of time how many minutes they will earn for appropriate behavior.

NAMES OF RESPONSIBLE STUDENTS ON BOARD

A number of substitute teachers have reported that this technique is very effective. Set it up by marking off space on the chalkboard and labeling it something like "Superstars." Periodically throughout the day, write the names of students who are behaving well. This is a system that does not require rewards—the honor of getting one's name on the board is itself the motivator. Some care should be taken when using this procedure, however.

First, make it clear that the students whose names are on the board are being rewarded. Some teachers make it a practice to put misbehaving students' names on the board.

Second, you need to be sure to get the name of every student who is following the rules on the board. It can be very easy to overlook the quiet or shy students.

Third, you should be prepared for the fact that you may need to remove a student's name from the list. If a student whose name is on the board misbehaves, give a warning: "If I have to remind you again about keeping your hands to yourself, I will have to erase your name from the board." If the misbehavior happens again, erase the student's name and inform her that if she behaves responsibly again for a significant period of time, she will be able to get her name back on the board.

for long-term substitutes

Ask for details about any motivation or reward systems that are already in place in the class where you'll be substituting. Students will expect those to continue (and will let you know about it if they don't). You may also want to implement additional systems if you think they will improve classroom behavior. You may adapt the systems above for longer periods of time—for example, reward students each time they accumulate a certain number of stars on the board. If they are earning 20–30 stars per day, have the target number start at 50. If the goal is set too high, students may not try to reach it. For additional reward and motivation systems, see *The Tough Kid Tool Box*, available in Fall 2009 from Pacific Northwest Publishing (www. pacificnwpublish.com).

PRINCIPLE 5:
CORRECT student misbehavior when it occurs.

Dealing with misbehavior is a challenge for every teacher, but it's often especially difficult for a substitute teacher. Students are more likely to test a substitute to see what they can get away with while their regular teacher is gone. The previous four principles of communicating, orchestrating, circulating, and motivating can prevent most misbehavior, but at some point a substitute will probably encounter a student who needs correction. Among the most important skills a substitute must have is knowing how to respond when students misbehave.

In general, correction should start with a mild (but firm) reprimand and progress gradually to more severe consequences only if necessary. For example, when a student misbehaves, inform the student that the behavior was unacceptable and explain why. "Kendra, please sit down. I cannot allow you to disturb other students."

If the behavior continues, warn the student that the next time you have to speak to her about the behavior, there will be a consequence. "Kendra, you need to return to your seat. This is the second time I have spoken to you about disturbing others. From this point on, you will lose one minute off the next recess for each time I have to remind you to stop."

If the student repeats the misbehavior, follow through and implement the consequence you identified.

The following information about correcting misbehavior is divided into two parts. The first part consists of five basic guidelines for correcting misbehavior. Those guidelines are:

- Correct calmly
- Correct consistently
- Correct fairly
- Correct immediately
- Correct as privately as possible

The second part identifies and describes specific consequences that you, as a substitute teacher, may be able to implement to correct misbehavior.

 ## Correct calmly.

Don't get physical. No matter what happens, do not touch a student while trying to correct misbehavior. It can be tempting to try to calm an angry student (or guide a noncompliant student) by putting a hand on the student's shoulder or taking the student by the arm. Under no circumstances should you do this. If a student refuses to do what you ask, such as go to the office, call for assistance from an administrator. Keep your hands to yourself at all times. This even extends to situations such as taking a toy away from a younger student.

> **No matter what happens, do not touch a student while trying to correct misbehavior.**

Let's say that a second-grade student is playing with a small toy car when he should be working on his assignments. You ask the student to put the car away, but he refuses. You then instruct the student to give the car to you and tell him you will return it at the end of the day. He simply keeps playing with the car. It does not seem inappropriate for you to take the car away from him. However, if doing so means that you have to touch the student, DON'T. The physical contact could lead to the student fighting with you over the car, and later the student could claim that you hurt him. Even if his claim is untrue, the chances are that you will not be asked to work in that school district again. A better response would be to say something like, "You need to put the car on the teacher's desk within the next two minutes. If you choose not to, I will have to send you to the office for refusing to follow my directions."

> *Your goal should always be to stay calm and simply let the student live with the consequences of her misbehavior.*

Don't escalate the situation. Part of correcting calmly is staying calm even when the student gets angry and/or tries to make you angry. Continuing with the toy car example, the student might try to engage you in an emotional argument. "It's my car and you can't take it from me!" Although it would be very easy to fall into such an argument with the student, you are much better off using the "broken record" technique. With this procedure, you respond to the student by repeating your instruction as many times as necessary, like a broken record. "You need to put the car on the teacher's desk within the next two minutes. If you choose not to, I will have to send you to the office for refusing to follow my directions." Each time the students tries to argue, simply repeat the original instruction.

Don't let the students smell blood. That is, even when you feel angry, worried, frightened, or in any other way upset, do not let the students see it. This has been discussed earlier, but it is especially critical when correcting misbehavior. When students see that they can rattle or upset you, it gives them status in front of their peers because they "battled" with an adult and won. Your goal should always be to stay calm and simply let the student live with the consequences of her misbehavior. You do not have to make the student behave—just let her know what the consequence will be (for example, being sent to the office for refusing to follow your direction) and stay calm.

Don't take it personally. The student is not misbehaving because of you. He would probably misbehave no matter who was in the classroom. If a student insults you, do not take offense; just implement a consequence for the disrespectful act. If you take things personally, you are likely to get upset, which will give the student power over you.

Don't worry about saving face. Most people, when they are insulted or their authority is threatened, tend to get angry. Just remember, when a student can get you angry, she has won. If a student does insult you, the other students may react at first as if they think it is exciting, but the truth is that they really do not want to see a battle between you and the student. What they need is to see that you are so confident and in control that you do not have to engage the student in a verbal battle. Simply state the choices and allow the student to live with the consequences of her actions.

Avoid power struggles. The most common type of power struggle in the classroom occurs when a teacher wants a student to do something that the student does not want to do. Although some power struggles may be unavoidable, you should definitely try to avoid unnecessary conflicts with students. The best strategy is to not ask a student to do something unimportant. If you ask, and the student refuses, you then have to decide whether to try to make him comply. Before giving an instruction, always think about whether it is truly important. Examples of important instructions related to misbehavior include telling a student to stop making noises while you are giving directions to the class, to stop poking and bothering other students, or to stop using profanity. If a student fails to stop any of these misbehaviors, it is reasonable to implement consequences, and the school administrator will probably support you.

An example of an unimportant instruction—one that could lead to an unnecessary power struggle—is telling a student to stop smirking while you are speaking to him. Consider the difficult position in which you place yourself if you give an instruction like, "Wipe that silly grin off your face right now!" What do you do if the student continues to grin? Send him to the office for grinning? This would create an awkward situation for both you and the school principal. The student can claim that he is being punished for just being happy. Before you give an instruction, always take time to ask yourself, "Is this important enough that the administrator will support me if the student refuses to follow my direction?"

 ## Correct consistently.

To effectively correct misbehavior, you need to be consistent. Examples of inconsistency include letting one student engage in a particular misbehavior but correcting the same misbehavior when another student engages in it, or giving a student a consequence for a particular misbehavior one time and later letting the same misbehavior go.

To be consistent requires that you give some thought ahead of time to the types of misbehaviors for which you will provide consequences and those that you will just let go. The basic concept here is to choose your battles carefully. As a general rule, if a student's misbehavior disrupts the learning process for others (such as loud noises, disruptive wisecracks, moving about the room, poking other students) or puts anyone in physical danger (such as hitting, tripping, jabbing with a pencil), you need to implement a consequence. When a student's behavior does not prevent others from learning, it is often better to just let it pass.

> " *To effectively correct misbehavior, you need to be consistent.* "

For example, if you are walking by and hear two students conversing and one quietly swears, but no other students hear, just keep walking. If a student is sitting doing nothing when he should be working, it is reasonable to ask the student to get to work. However, if he chooses not to, it is probably not worth trying to apply a consequence as long as he is not disturbing other students.

Consistency also requires that you assign consequences that you can follow through on. For example, don't threaten students with what the teacher will do to them when he or she gets back because this is not something that you can implement (and it puts the teacher in an unreasonable position). Another example might be telling a student that she has to stay after school. If the student rides the bus, this consequence is unenforceable. When you threaten a student with unknown consequences ("If you do that again, you'll wish you were never born!"), it is very likely that the student will recognize it as an empty threat. If the student does misbehave again, what will you do? When warning about consequences, mention only those that you know you will be able to apply.

 ## Correct fairly.

Students (like most of us) are very sensitive to fairness. When they believe that you are fair in implementing consequences, they are more likely to respect you for dealing with the misbehavior of a few students. However, if they feel that you are unfair, you risk not only losing the respect of all the students but also losing control of the class.

One of the most important rules of fairness is: Don't punish the whole class for the behavior of one or two students. It is not fair to the students who are behaving well to say, "If Jerome and Charlie continue to be disruptive, everyone will be held after class." The rest of the students do not have the power to control the behavior of their peers and should not be punished if these individuals choose to misbehave.

> *Don't punish the whole class for the behavior of one or two students.*

Another guideline about fairness is that once you have implemented a consequence for a misbehavior with one student, you must be prepared to apply it to any other student who behaves the same way. Students need to know that you are not out to get certain individuals. If you implement a consequence when Gina is disruptive, but do not implement the same consequence when Robert is disruptive, students will feel that you are being unfair (and they will be right!).

 ## Correct immediately.

When a misbehavior disrupts the learning process for others, do not let it go. Do something as soon as the behavior becomes a problem. If you allow it to continue, the student will think that the behavior is acceptable to you. The first time an unacceptable behavior occurs, inform the student that the behavior is unacceptable. If it happens again, inform the student that he has a choice: Continue the behavior and live with the consequence (which you should specifically define), or behave responsibly. Thereafter, follow through with the consequence you identified.

Correct as privately as possible.

When a student is misbehaving, the most effective way to correct is to go to the student and in a reasonably quiet voice inform her that the behavior is unacceptable. This may not be completely private. Students sitting near the misbehaving student may be able to hear you, but students across the room should not. A semiprivate interaction allows the student to save face. Correcting the student in a public voice that everyone in the room can hear may embarrass her in front of the class. She may end up feeling obligated to misbehave in order to demonstrate that she is not afraid of you. Correcting privately, or at least in a quiet voice, demonstrates both to the misbehaving student and to the other students that you are not trying to embarrass her with your correction.

POSSIBLE CONSEQUENCES

The following five consequences are reasonable for a substitute teacher to use with students who misbehave. They range from mild to severe. In general, you should use the mildest consequence that fits the infraction. For example, if a student makes a sarcastic remark, a reprimand is probably the most appropriate consequence. If the behavior continues, a more severe consequence (for example, having to stay after class for 30 seconds for each infraction after the warning) is warranted. Sending a student to the office should be reserved for those times when a student engages in a very serious misbehavior, such as overtly refusing to follow one of your instructions. Avoid using any consequence that involves academic tasks—for example, requiring the student to write sentences or complete extra math problems. Teachers and administrators will generally not want you to use academic work as a consequence for misbehavior.

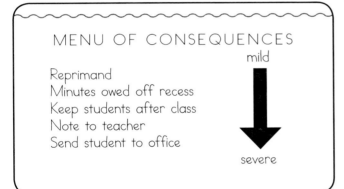

MENU OF CONSEQUENCES

mild

Reprimand
Minutes owed off recess
Keep students after class
Note to teacher
Send student to office

severe

Before the day begins, you should have these possible consequences in mind so that you will be ready to implement them as necessary. If this is the first time you are working in a particular building, it might be worth asking the building administrator if he or she approves of these consequences.

REPRIMAND

A reprimand is a simple statement that the student's behavior is unacceptable. It should clearly inform the student that she is engaged in misbehavior, and it should specify what she should be doing instead. "Judy, those noises are distracting to me and to others in the class. You need to sit quietly without making noises." This should be the first thing you try with most misbehaviors. If the behavior continues, warn the student that she will have to pay a consequence (see examples that follow) if she chooses to continue the misbehavior.

MINUTES OWED OFF RECESS

This consequence is useful in elementary classrooms. After giving both a reprimand and a warning, advise the student that from that point on, each time he repeats the infraction, he will owe you one minute from recess time. "Allen, I have given a warning about disturbing others. You have now lost one minute of recess time, and you need to go back to your seat."

If the student again starts to bother others, inform him that you are taking away another minute of recess. Be sure to write down each occurrence so that when recess comes you can follow through.

"Class, it is time for recess. Allen owes two minutes and Zoe owes one. Everyone else please line up."

During the time owed, have the students sit quietly at their desks. When the time is up, excuse the students and let them know that you are sure they will behave more appropriately for the rest of the day.

"Zoe, your time is paid. You may go out to recess. I am looking forward to seeing you after recess, and I am sure that you will remember the rule about treating people respectfully."

KEEP STUDENTS AFTER CLASS

In secondary schools, where students do not have recesses, you can use a variation of time owed. First, reprimand the student. Then, if the behavior continues, warn the student that repeated infractions will lead you to keep her after class. If it happens again, plan on keeping the student after class for 30 seconds. If there's another infraction, assign another 30 seconds. You should not keep anyone longer than one minute after class, because it is unfair to the student's next period teacher to make the student late. Therefore, after two infractions, tell the student that should the behavior occur again, she will not owe time, but will be sent to the office.

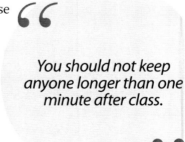

You should not keep anyone longer than one minute after class.

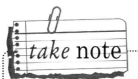

When only one student owes time, keep the classroom door open. You might even want to stand in the doorway so that you can be seen by students and teachers who pass by the room. This is to avoid any appearance that you have the student alone behind closed doors. Although it is unlikely, should the student later claim that you hit or touched him or her in an inappropriate manner, you will have witnesses who saw you standing in the doorway, nowhere close to the student.

NOTE TO TEACHER

With some misbehaviors, you may wish to let the student know that if the behavior continues, you will leave a note for the classroom teacher. As previously stated, you never want to threaten the student with what the teacher will do (because you don't know), but it is reasonable to leave a note that describes exactly what the student did.

A variation of this consequence is to write the note and instruct the student to sign it. For some students, being required to sign the note will make the whole interaction seem much more official. However, if you think that making the student sign the note will cause more conflict, do not use this procedure.

SEND STUDENT TO OFFICE

For severe misbehaviors, such as physically dangerous acts, seriously disruptive behavior, or overt defiance to your authority, plan to send the student to the office. Before you begin the school day, be sure to find out from an administrator or from the office personnel what the school's procedures are in this regard. Some schools have teachers deal with very disruptive students by sending them to another classroom or resource room instead of to the principal's office. Find out if you need to fill out a form or a report. Do you need to call the office on the intercom and inform them that a student is on the way? If you know exactly what the procedures are, you will be more confident should you have to employ this consequence.

Do not send a student to the office for trivial problems. Minor disruptions should be handled with less severe consequences. However, when one student repeatedly engages in disruptive behavior, warn that student that the next time you have to speak to him, he will be sent to the office. "Adam, that is disruptive. You now owe five minutes off recess. If I have to speak to you again, I will send you to the office and inform the principal that I have had to speak to you more than seven times about being disruptive."

QUICK REVIEW: CHAPTER 3

Principle 1: COMMUNICATE with the students.

» Share your expectations for student behavior at the beginning of the day (or class).

- Use the teacher's posted rules when possible.
- Have your own rules in mind in case there are none posted. Limit your rules to three or four, state them positively, and give students a rationale for them.

» During the day (or class), interact with students as much as possible.

Principle 2: ORCHESTRATE student behavior during and between activities.

» Begin each activity by clarifying your expectations for student behavior during that activity.

» End each activity by giving the class feedback on how well they met your expectations and by preparing them for the next activity.

Principle 3: CIRCULATE throughout the classroom.

» Move among the students as much as possible.

» Be unpredictable in your route when circulating.

» Visually scan the entire classroom as frequently as possible.

Principle 4: MOTIVATE students to follow the rules and to use time productively.

≫ Use praise frequently and appropriately. Effective praise is:
- Descriptive
- Based on something important
- Age-appropriate
- Businesslike
- Reasonably private (for older students)

≫ Let the students know that you will be reporting back to their teacher.

≫ Reinforcement systems may be useful with younger students (K–4):
- Self-monitoring form
- Stars or points on the board
- "Good Work" certificates
- Mystery Motivators
- Names of responsible students on the board (use with care)

Principle 5: CORRECT student misbehavior when it occurs.

≫ Correct calmly.
≫ Correct consistently.
≫ Correct fairly.
≫ Correct immediately.
≫ Correct privately.

Notes

Chapter 4

YOU CAN LEARN MANY THINGS FROM CHILDREN. HOW MUCH
PATIENCE YOU HAVE, FOR INSTANCE.
••• *Franklin P. Jones*

DEALING WITH PREDICTABLE EVENTS

*S*choolchildren of every generation think they have invented new ways to confuse and embarrass substitute teachers. Actually, generations of students have been using the same ploys, so they can rightly be called "Predictable Events." You probably remember the following situations from your own days as a student.

That's Not How Our Teacher Does It!

This is a very common thing for a substitute teacher to hear. Because you know it is likely to come up, you might want to precorrect: Talk to students at the beginning of the day about it. After introducing yourself, let the students know that because you don't know all the classroom routines, some things you do will be different from how their regular teacher does them, and that is OK. You might say something like:

for example

Because I am not sure how Mrs. Hernandez does things, I will probably do some things differently. Occasionally I may ask for your help. For example, in just a minute I will need to know how Mrs. Hernandez takes attendance, does lunch count, and handles the calendar activity. When I ask for help, I want you to raise your hand and wait to be called on. If I call on you, tell me how Mrs. Hernandez conducts these activities.

There will be other times today when I use my own way of doing things, ways that may not be what you are used to. I hope that you will be flexible and willing to try doing things a little bit differently today. Now, raise your hand if you can tell me . . .

Later, if students try to help by telling you how their regular teacher does things (and there are not too many of these comments), thank the students for their suggestions and try to do things in a fairly similar way. If, however, you receive too many suggestions, or suggestions that are silly, or even a suggestion that just does not fit the way you want to do things, simply say, "Thanks for those suggestions, but this time let's do it a little differently. Let's . . ."

> "When a student or class gives you lots of obviously unrealistic comments about how the teacher does things, try humor."

When a student or class pushes the issue, giving you lots of obviously unrealistic comments about how the teacher does things, try humor. "I think I will start making notes on all these helpful reminders about how your teacher does things. I'm looking forward to asking Mrs. Hernandez about some of these very interesting techniques." The next time a student gives one of these "suggestions," tell the students that this is an example of the suggestions you want to ask the teacher about and write it down. This will usually stop the problem.

Changing Seats

When students (particularly middle school students) know in advance that they are going to have a substitute, they may prearrange to switch seats, making the seating chart inaccurate. You can usually tell that this has occurred because students will be snickering and calling each other by their "wrong" names in exaggerated ways.

> *How are you today, Barry?*
>
> *Just fine, Ruth. How are you?*

If you think this has happened, try to handle it with a smile and a bit of humor. You can let the students know that you will be using the seating chart, so if they don't want to pay the consequences for someone else's actions, they may want to move to their own seats. From that point on, use the seating chart.

If the problem continues and/or becomes disruptive, wait until the next break, then go and ask an administrator or co-teacher to stop by the room and verify the accuracy of the seating chart. Usually this will not be necessary, but keep it in mind if the situation becomes too much of a problem.

Also try humor with the student who says his name is something different than what you have on the chart.

> *for* example
>
> If a student says his name is "George Washington" and the chart says "Travis Smith," you might say something like, "Well, George, I have trouble with names, so I'm going to call you Travis because that's what's on the seating chart. I hope that's OK."

Class Clown

Some classes have one student who views herself as the class comedian. This student may tell jokes or make sarcastic remarks to get other students to laugh. There are several strategies for handling this very predictable situation. The first is to do nothing: Let the student make jokes, let the class laugh, and simply keep going with the next activity. It's possible that if you ignore the behavior, the student will stop. Of course, if the student's goal is to get you to try to make her stop, she may actually increase the behavior until it becomes a mildly disruptive influence if you don't respond. Still, the best policy when the behavior is mild is to ignore it.

Another strategy that works for some, but not all, substitute teachers is to use humor. When you can laugh at the student's comments and make a humorous comment in return, you often earn the respect of both that student and the rest of the class. It is important, however, never to use humor in a manner that embarrasses or insults a student. In addition to being unkind and inappropriate, sarcasm or ridicule can lead to a power struggle between you and the student, with both of you competing to see who can top the other in an effort to get the attention of the class.

> *You want the student to know that you are recording his actions and comments.*

Another strategy is to win the student to your side. That is, sometime after the student has behaved inappropriately, ask him to assist you with a task. For example, you might ask this student and another student to pass out papers or take a note to the office. A simple request like this demonstrates that you do not hold a grudge and that you respect the student enough to ask for his help.

If the problem is too severe to ignore or to respond to with humor (for example, the student's comments are cruel to others or overtly disrespectful to you), keep anecdotal notes. That is, each time the student makes an inappropriate comment, take a moment and write a description of what was said. Be specific, and quote the student as accurately as possible. Do not try to hide the fact that you are keeping these notes. You want the student to know that you are recording his actions and comments.

If the student asks what you are going to do with the notes, inform him that if the behavior persists, you may need to share the notes with the regular teacher and/or the building administrator. When you have a break between classes, take the notes to the administrator.

Class Out of Control

One of the most terrifying situations for any substitute teacher is to have a class that is out of control and not know what to do. Any time the noise level is too high or students are otherwise too disruptive, go to the front of the room, raise your hand in the air, and firmly say, "Class, I need your attention, please."

If they don't respond, don't shout and don't get upset—just wait. If you shout for the students to be silent, you set up a situation in which you may have to repeatedly shout to get their attention. A better strategy is to keep your hand in the air and repeat your instruction in a firm (but not shouting) voice. If students still do not settle down, check the clock and write the time on the chalkboard. Then raise your hand again and continue to wait.

Once student behavior is under control, check the time again and write it on the board above the first time. Subtract the first recorded time from the second and write the number of minutes on the board. Explain to the class that they just spent x minutes behaving unacceptably. Tell them that the next time you ask for their attention and they do not give it to you within a few seconds, you will repeat this process and will inform their teacher and/or the principal how many minutes they chose to behave in this manner.

If this is the first out-of-control episode, you may then wish to say that you doubt the class will have the problem again, so you will not share this incident with either the teacher or the administrator. Then erase the times from the board. However, if the situation does arise again, be sure that the class knows that you are recording the amount of time it takes for them to respond to your direction to pay attention.

> "Ask for attention, raise your hand, and, if necessary, record the time it takes for the class to respond."

Do not use this procedure when only a few (four or fewer) students are failing to pay attention. If a small group is misbehaving in a way that makes it impossible for you to get the attention of the rest of the class, write the names of those individuals on the board, then record the time. Wait until those students are paying attention to you, record that time, and then figure out the number of minutes involved. Inform those individual students that for any further incidents, you will calculate the amount of time they are not paying attention and they will owe you that much time off the next recess. At the secondary level, inform the students that they will owe you time after class. If the accumulated time is greater than one minute, you will have to refer them to the office.

Sometimes a class will conspire to rattle the sub. For example, a group of middle school students may have planned before class to all start tapping their pencils at the same time. If something like this happens, use this same technique: Ask for attention, raise your hand, and, if necessary, record the time it takes for the class to respond. The technique can be used for any situation in which a group of students is engaged in misbehavior, or even with a group of elementary students who are having trouble settling down after they return from recess.

by Dave Carpenter, www.CartoonStock.com

"This is the fifth 'get well' card this week from your substituting teacher.

QUICK REVIEW: DEALING WITH PREDICTABLE EVENTS

That's Not How Our Teacher Does It

» Precorrect: "Today, I will try to do some things like Ms. Hernandez does, but some things will be different. I hope you will be patient about this."

» Thank helpful students and try to use some of their suggestions, if possible.

» Don't confront students who seem to be playing games. Try humor if they are insistent.

Changing Seats

» Give a warning that you will be following the seating chart for all activities, including any times that you may have to assign consequences.

» When a student gives a name that is clearly different from what is on the seating chart, try humor.

» When you are not sure, ask an administrator or co-teacher to verify the accuracy of the seating chart and the seating arrangements.

Class Clown

» Use humor, but do not humiliate or alienate the student.

» Get the student on your side (e.g., ask him to help you with a task).

» Keep anecdotal notes if the problem continues. Let the student know that you will share the notes with the teacher and/or an administrator if the behavior persists.

Class Out of Control

Ask for attention and raise your hand in the air. If students do not respond, check the time and write it on the board. Once class is under control, again check the time and write it on the board. Calculate the difference (i.e., the amount of time the class was out of control.) Warn the class, then leave a note for the teacher if the problem recurs.

Chapter 5

FINALLY, IN CONCLUSION, LET ME SAY JUST THIS.
••• *Peter Sellers*

CONCLUSION

Remember that you, the substitute teacher, play a very important role in the educational process. The most important things to keep in mind about doing your job successfully are:

- No matter what happens, maintain the appearance of calm and confidence.

- Greet students at the classroom door so that you can set a positive tone immediately.

- Implement the essentials of managing student behavior: Communicate, Orchestrate, Circulate, Motivate, and Correct.

PRINCIPLES OF BEHAVIOR MANAGEMENT

1. COMMUNICATE with students. Develop three or four general behavioral rules, clarify procedures for following the rules, and enforce the rules.

> "Students cannot know what you expect or how you think they are doing unless you communicate with them."

2. ORCHESTRATE student behavior during and between activities. Clarify your expectations for student behavior, give feedback to students about their behavior, and end each activity by preparing them for the next activity.

3. CIRCULATE throughout the classroom. Move among the students as much as possible, be unpredictable in your movements, and visually scan the classroom frequently.

4. MOTIVATE students to follow the rules and use their time productively. Use descriptive praise frequently and appropriately for the age group. Let students know that you will be reporting back to their teacher. Use reinforcement systems with younger students. They may also be successful with middle school students.

5. CORRECT student misbehavior when it occurs. Correct calmly, consistently, fairly, immediately, and as privately as possible.

"I'll have the decaf. Twenty-one second graders will provide me with enough stimulation."

REFERENCES

Augustin, H. (1987). Substitute teachers: An endangered species. *The Clearing House, 60*(9), 393–396.

Benedict, K. C. (1987). Student expectations and the substitute teacher. *The Clearing House, 61*(1), 27–28.

Brace, D. L. (1990). Establishing a support system for substitute teachers. *NASSP Bulletin, 74*(526), 73–77.

Clifton, R. A., & Rambaran, R. (1987). Substitute teaching: Survival in a marginal situation. *Urban Education, 22*(3), 310–327.

Collins, S. H. (1984). *The effective substitute teacher.* Eugene, OR: Garlic Press.

Drury, W. R. (1988). Eight ways to make sure substitute teachers aren't babysitters. *American School Board Journal, 175*(3), 51.

Glatfelter, A. G. (2006). Substitute teachers as effective classroom instructors (Doctoral dissertation, University of California, Los Angeles, 2006). (ERIC Document Reproduction Service No. ED 494940)

Gresham, J., Donihoo, J., & Cox, T. (2007). 5 strategies to enhance your substitute teaching. *Kappa Delta Pi Record, 44*(1) 28–32.

Jenson, W. R., Rhode, G., & Reavis, H. K. (1994, in press). *The tough kid tool box: A collection of classroom tools.* Eugene, OR: Pacific Northwest Publishing.

Jones, K. R. (1999). Managing substitute teaching. *NAESP Here's How, 18*(2), 2–5.

Kraft, D. W. (1980). New approaches to the substitute teacher problem. *NASSP Bulletin, 64*(437), 79–86.

Nelson, M. (1983). A few steps by regular teachers can help substitutes with class instruction. *NASSP Bulletin, 67*(466), 98–100.

Platt, J. M. (1987). Substitute teachers can do more than just keep the lid on. *Teaching Exceptional Children, 19*(2), 28–31.

Pronin, B. (1983). Guerrilla guide to effective substitute teaching. *Instructor, 92*(6), 64–66, 68.

Purvis, J. R., & Garvey, R. C. (1993). Components of an effective substitute teacher program. *The Clearing House, 66*(6), 370–373.

Rhode, G., Jenson, W. R., & Reavis, H. K. (1992). *The tough kid book: Practical classroom management strategies.* Eugene, OR: Pacific Northwest Publishing. Second edition available 2010.

Shreeve, W. C., Nicely-Leach, J., Radebaugh, M. R., Morrill, C. M., & Slatton, S. (1983). *Substitute teachers: The professional contradiction.* (Report No. SP 028 444). Cheney, WA: Eastern Washington University. (ERIC Document Reproduction Service No. ED 278621)

Simmons, B. J. (1991). Planning to improve the quality of the substitute teacher program. *NASSP Bulletin, 72*(531), 91–98.

Sprick, R. (2009). *CHAMPS: A proactive and positive approach to classroom management* (2nd ed.). Eugene, OR: Pacific Northwest Publishing.

Stanley, S. (1991). Substitute teachers can manage their classrooms effectively. *NASSP Bulletin, 75*(532), 84–88.

Substitute Teachers Caucus of the National Education Association, Substitute Educators Day, Nov. 21, 2003. Retrieved October 2, 2008, from http://www.substituteteachers.org/sed.html

Sykes, S. (October 24, 2002). Substitutes teach 6.4 percent of classroom time. *The Salt Lake Tribune*, p. B3.

Tracy, S. J. (1988). Improve substitute teaching with staff development. *NASSP Bulletin, 72*(508), 85–88.

Utah State University (2009). *Substitute teacher handbook: Proven professional management skills and teaching strategies* (7th ed.). Logan, UT: Substitute Teaching Training Institute, Utah State University.

Warren, R. (1988). Substitute teachers—Education's relief pitchers. *NASSP Bulletin, 72*(512), 96–99.

APPENDIX

REPRODUCIBLE FORMS

This appendix contains blank blackline master versions of all Reproducible Forms that appear in this book. Permission is given to educators who purchase this book to reproduce any form labeled "Reproducible Form" solely for classroom use.

A companion book, *Structuring Success for Substitutes: A Guide for Administrators and Teachers*, includes a CD with many of these forms in PDF format. They can be printed and filled out by hand. They are also enabled so they can be filled out and saved electronically when opened in Adobe Reader version 6 or above.

REPRODUCIBLE FORMS

1.1a School Information for Substitute Teachers, Elementary	**2.1c** End-of-Day Report, Secondary
1.1b School Information for Substitute Teachers, Secondary	**3.1** How'd We Do? (Monitoring Class Behavior)
1.2 Hall Passes	**3.2** How'd I Do? (Monitoring Student Behavior)
2.1a End-of-Day Report, Elementary (Version 1)	**3.3** Good Work Certificates
2.1b End-of-Day Report, Elementary (Version 2)	**3.4** Mystery Motivator

SCHOOL INFORMATION FOR SUBSTITUTE TEACHERS, ELEMENTARY

School: Phone:

Address/Directions:

Contacts

☐ Key front-office personnel:

☐ Teachers (and room numbers) who can answer questions:

☐ How to use the intercom and/or contact another teacher or administrator while in class:

Schedules

☐ School schedule:

Overview of teacher's weekly schedule and responsibilities, including:

    ☐ Recess duty:

    ☐ Lunch duty:

    ☐ Bus duty:

    ☐ Other:

☐ Schedule of daily activities and classes:

☐ Assembly schedule and procedures:

Classroom information

Location of:

☐ Lesson plans:

☐ Backup lesson plans and activities:

☐ Copy machine (password or key code and copy allotment):

☐ AV equipment/procedures:

☐ Map of classroom and school:

☐ Seating charts:

☐ Student roster/information about individual students:

Classroom information (*continued*)

☐ Students designated as classroom hosts:

☐ Classroom helpers (student teachers, paraprofessionals, or parents who may be in the classroom):

Descriptions of classroom routines:

☐ Attendance procedure:

☐ Lunch count:

☐ Dismissal procedure:

☐ Other:

☐ Teacher's expectations for grading papers, cleaning room, feeding animals, etc.:

☐ After-school responsibilities:

☐ Emergency procedures (e.g., fire drills, medical emergencies, lockdowns):

Reports

☐ End-of-Day Report form or explanation of how the substitute is to provide feedback about the day's activities

☐ Copy of substitute evaluation form (administrator or teacher to fill out)

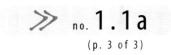
Rules

☐ Summaries of classroom discipline and motivation/reward systems and any schoolwide discipline policies/procedures:

Policies/procedures for common situations:

☐ Hall passes:

☐ Cell phone/pager use:

☐ Personal electronics use (laptops, MP3 players, etc.):

☐ Restroom use:

☐ Drinking fountain use:

☐ Pencil sharpener use:

☐ Acceptable free-time activities:

☐ Recess procedures for rainy days:

☐ Recess protocol:

☐ Students in room before and after school:

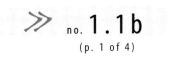
SCHOOL INFORMATION FOR SUBSTITUTE TEACHERS, SECONDARY

School:

Address:

Directions:

Contacts

☐ Key front-office personnel:

☐ Teachers (and room numbers) who can answer questions:

☐ How to use the intercom and/or contact another teacher or administrator while in class:

Schedules

☐ School schedule:

Overview of teacher's weekly schedule and responsibilities, including:

☐ Recess duty:

☐ Lunch duty:

☐ Bus duty:

☐ Other:

☐ Schedule of daily activities and classes:

☐ Assembly schedule and procedures:

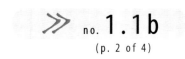
Classroom information

Location of:

☐ Lesson plans:

☐ Backup lesson plans and activities:

☐ Copy machine (password or key code and copy allotment):

☐ AV equipment (and procedures):

☐ Map of classroom and school:

☐ Seating charts:

☐ Student roster and information about individual students:

☐ Students designated as classroom hosts:

☐ Classroom helpers (student teachers, paraprofessionals, or parents who may be in the classroom):

Descriptions of classroom routines:

☐ Attendance procedure:

☐ Lunch count:

☐ Dismissal procedure:

☐ Other:

Classroom information (*continued*)

☐ Teacher's expectations for grading papers, cleaning room, feeding animals, etc.:

☐ After-school responsibilities:

☐ Emergency procedures (e.g., fire drills, medical emergencies, lockdowns):

Reports

☐ End-of-Day Report form or explanation of how the substitute is to provide feedback about the day's activities

☐ Copy of substitute evaluation form (administrator or teacher to fill out)

Rules

☐ Summaries of classroom discipline and motivation/reward systems and any schoolwide discipline policies/procedures:

Policies/procedures for common situations:

☐ Hall passes:

☐ Cell phone/pager use:

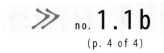
Rules (*continued*)

☐ Personal electronics use (laptops, MP3 players, etc.):

☐ Restroom use:

☐ Drinking fountain use:

☐ Pencil sharpener use:

☐ Acceptable free-time activities:

☐ Recess procedures for rainy days:

☐ Recess protocol:

☐ Students in room before and after school:

Other Information

HALL PASSES

HALL PASS

Student: _____

Time: _____

Destination: _____

Teacher: _____

Subbing for: _____ Room: _____

HALL PASS

Student: _____

Time: _____

Destination: _____

Teacher: _____

Subbing for: _____ Room: _____

HALL PASS

Student: _____

Time: _____

Destination: _____

Teacher: _____

Subbing for: _____ Room: _____

HALL PASS

Student: _____

Time: _____

Destination: _____

Teacher: _____

Subbing for: _____ Room: _____

HALL PASS

Student: _____

Time: _____

Destination: _____

Teacher: _____

Subbing for: _____ Room: _____

HALL PASS

Student: _____

Time: _____

Destination: _____

Teacher: _____

Subbing for: _____ Room: _____

HALL PASS

Student: _____

Time: _____

Destination: _____

Teacher: _____

Subbing for: _____ Room: _____

HALL PASS

Student: _____

Time: _____

Destination: _____

Teacher: _____

Subbing for: _____ Room: _____

HALL PASS

Student: _____

Time: _____

Destination: _____

Teacher: _____

Subbing for: _____ Room: _____

HALL PASS

Student: _____

Time: _____

Destination: _____

Teacher: _____

Subbing for: _____ Room: _____

END-OF-DAY REPORT, ELEMENTARY (Version 1)

Substitute Teacher: _____

Classroom Teacher: _____ Date: _____

Time: _____ Activity: _____ This is what we did: Special circumstances or problems:	Absent students: Student behavior was: _____ Excellent! _____ Average _____ Unacceptable (describe in box at left)
Time: _____ Activity: _____ This is what we did: Special circumstances or problems:	Absent students: Student behavior was: _____ Excellent! _____ Average _____ Unacceptable (describe in box at left)
Time: _____ Activity: _____ This is what we did: Special circumstances or problems:	Absent students: Student behavior was: _____ Excellent! _____ Average _____ Unacceptable (describe in box at left)

END-OF-DAY REPORT, ELEMENTARY (Version 2)

Substitute Teacher: _____

Classroom Teacher: _____ Date: _____

Students who were absent (include part-day absences):

Students who were especially helpful (provide specifics):

Students who had trouble behaving appropriately (provide details):

Description of what occurred during each of the main activities of the day (academic work and student behavior):

Activity:	Activity:
Activity:	Activity:
Activity:	Activity:
Activity:	Activity:

STEPPING IN
A Substitute's Guide to Managing Classroom Behavior

≫ no. 2.1c

END-OF-DAY REPORT, SECONDARY

Substitute Teacher: _____

Classroom Teacher: _____ Date: _____

For each period of the day, please thoroughly describe what was accomplished. Also note which students were absent, which students were particularly helpful, and which students behaved inappropriately (be as specific as you reasonably can). Use an extra sheet of paper for additional comments, if needed.

Period 1:
Period 2:
Period 3:
Period 4:
Period 5:
Period 6:
Period 7:
Comments:

HOW'D WE DO? (MONITORING CLASS BEHAVIOR)

After each major activity (listed down the left side), circle the number that best represents how the class behaved during that activity.

Time	Activity	Behavior needed improvement.	Some students behaved responsibly.	Most students behaved responsibly.	All students behaved responsibly.
		0	1	2	3
		0	1	2	3
		0	1	2	3
		0	1	2	3
		0	1	2	3
		0	1	2	3
		0	1	2	3
		0	1	2	3

Notes:

Substitute Teacher: _____

Classroom Teacher: _____ Date: _____

HOW'D I DO? (MONITORING STUDENT BEHAVIOR)

Student: _____ Date: _____

After each major activity (listed down the left side), circle the number that best represents how you behaved during that activity.

Time	Activity	My behavior needed improvement.	I behaved responsibly some of the time.	I behaved responsibly most of the time.	I behaved responsibly all of the time.
		0	1	2	3
		0	1	2	3
		0	1	2	3
		0	1	2	3
		0	1	2	3
		0	1	2	3
		0	1	2	3
		0	1	2	3

GOOD WORK CERTIFICATES

Good Work Certificate

_____

has done a fine job of behaving responsibly
and working hard!

Good Work Certificate

_____

has done a fine job of behaving responsibly
and working hard!

Good Work Certificate

_____

has done a fine job of behaving responsibly
and working hard!

Good Work Certificate

_____

has done a fine job of behaving responsibly
and working hard!

Good Work Certificate

_____

has done a fine job of behaving responsibly
and working hard!

Good Work Certificate

_____

has done a fine job of behaving responsibly
and working hard!

Good Work Certificate

_____

has done a fine job of behaving responsibly
and working hard!

Good Work Certificate

_____

has done a fine job of behaving responsibly
and working hard!

Good Work Certificate

_____

has done a fine job of behaving responsibly
and working hard!

Good Work Certificate

_____

has done a fine job of behaving responsibly
and working hard!

Good Work Certificate

_____

has done a fine job of behaving responsibly
and working hard!

Good Work Certificate

_____

has done a fine job of behaving responsibly
and working hard!

MYSTERY MOTIVATOR

1st Hour	2nd Hour	3rd Hour	4th Hour	5th Hour	6th Hour	7th Hour	BONUS

Name: _____

Comments: _____

_____

_____

_____

Adapted from *The Tough Kid Tool Box* by William R. Jenson, Ginger Rhode, and H. Kenton Reavis (1994, 2009).
Available from Pacific Northwest Publishing, www.pacificnwpublish.com. Reprinted with permission.

The Tough Kid Series

WILLIAM R. JENSON, PH.D., GINGER RHODE PH.D., AND COLLEAGUES

Constant and intense aggression, arguing, tantrums, noncompliance, and poor academic progress—these are characteristic of the Tough Kid. You can't "cure" Tough Kids, but you can use proactive, positive techniques to manage and motivate them. Effective management will help your Tough Kids succeed in school and make life in your classroom easier for you and for the other students.

The Tough Kid Book (2nd ed.) is for regular and special education teachers, counselors, instructional coaches, and any educator who wants effective and positively focused classrooms. Learn how to structure your classroom to ensure success for Tough Kids and use practical techniques for managing difficult students.

042-9 978-1-59909-042-9 / 2010 / 256 pp. and 1 CD of fillable reproducible forms

Visit the Pacific Northwest Publishing web site at www.pacificnwpublish.com for more details about other titles in The Tough Kid Series.

Teach All, Reach All: Instructional Design & Delivery With TGIF!

SUSAN L. MULKEY, M.ED., KAREN A. KEMP, M.A.

If you are serious about filling your bag of tricks with proven ideas, this is the instructional strategy book for you. *Teach All, Reach All* provides more than 175 practical classroom strategies with a companion CD of reproducible forms, plus a reproducible form to guide effective lesson design. This book is about high-quality instruction and interventions that are available for all students and grade levels. *Teach All, Reach All* complements the fundamental premise of RTI.

029-0 978-1-59909-029-0 / 2009 / 240 pp. and 1 CD of reproducible forms

CHAMPS (2nd ed.): A Proactive and Positive Approach to Classroom Management

RANDY SPRICK, PH.D.

CHAMPS helps classroom teachers design or fine-tune a proactive and positive classroom management plan that will overtly teach students how to behave responsibly. *CHAMPS* strategies are easy to implement and will:

- Reduce classroom disruptions and office referrals
- Improve classroom climate
- Increase student on-task behavior
- Establish respectful and civil interactions

030-6 978-1-59909-030-6 / 2009 / 520 pp. and 1 CD with 502 fillable reproducible forms and classroom icons)

Discipline in the Secondary Classroom (2nd ed.) A Positive Approach to Behavior Management

RANDY SPRICK, PH.D.

Discipline in the Secondary Classroom gives teachers in grades 9–12 step-by-step guidance for designing a behavior management plan that will help prevent misbehavior and increase student motivation. The book is a hands-on resource that contains easy-to-implement strategies distilled from a research-based approach. Forms, samples, and evaluation tools help teachers continually fine-tune their management plan.

226-7 978-0-470-42226-7 / 2006 / 286 pp. and 1 DVD of video clips and fillable reproducible forms

New! Teacher Planners based on the *CHAMPS/Discipline in the Secondary Classroom* approach to classroom management. Find out more at www.PacificNWPublish.com